British Railw

D
MULTIPLE UNITS

THIRTY-SEVENTH EDITION
2024

The complete guide to all Diesel Multiple Units
and On-Track Machines which operate on the
national railway network

Robert Pritchard

ISBN 978 1915 984 11 1

© 2023. Platform 5 Publishing Ltd, 52 Broadfield Road, Sheffield, S8 0XJ,
England.

Printed in England by The Lavenham Press, Lavenham, Suffolk.

CONTENTS

PROVISION OF INFORMATION

This book has been compiled with care to be as accurate as possible, but some information is not easily available and the publisher cannot be held responsible for any errors or omissions. We would like to thank the companies and individuals who have been helpful in supplying information to us. The authors of this series of books are always pleased to receive notification of any inaccuracies that may be found, to enhance future editions. Please send comments to:

Robert Pritchard, Platform 5 Publishing Ltd, 52 Broadfield Road, Sheffield, S8 0XJ, England.

e-mail: robert.pritchard@platform5.com Tel: 0114 255 2625.

This book is updated to information received by 16 October 2023.

UPDATES

This book is updated to the Stock Changes given in **Today's Railways UK 261** (November 2023). The Platform 5 railway magazine **"Today's Railways UK"** publishes Stock Changes every month to update this book. The magazine also contains news and rolling stock information on the railways of Great Britain and is published on the second Monday of every month. For further details of **Today's Railways UK**, please contact Platform 5 Publishing Ltd or visit our website **www.platform5.com**.

Front cover photograph: East Midlands Railway-liveried 170273 passes Wilmorton, Derby with the 11.10 Crewe–Newark Castle on 18 April 2023.　　**Tom McAtee**

BRITAIN'S RAILWAY SYSTEM

The structure of Britain's railway system has changed significantly during recent years, following the ongoing Covid-19 pandemic and subsequent drop in passenger numbers. Although passengers have since been returning in numbers, that drop in passengers in 2020 meant that franchises were no longer profitable and the Government was forced to step in and provide financial support to operators. Initially in March 2020 the Transport Secretary suspended rail franchising and operators transitioned to "Emergency Measures Agreements". These EMAs suspended the normal financial agreements, instead transferring all revenue and cost risk to the Government. Operators in England all accepted these new arrangements and continued to operate trains (initially with reduced service frequencies) for a small management fee. Similar arrangements were put in place by the Scottish and Welsh Governments for ScotRail, Caledonian Sleeper and Transport for Wales.

The EMAs initially lasted for six months from which time longer "Emergency Recovery Management Agreements" (ERMAs) were put in place. These were similar management contracts which continued to see operators run services for a management fee. Since then operators have been transitioning to new National Rail Contracts (NRCs). During an NRC operators are paid a fixed management fee of around 1.5% for operating services and additional small performance fees if agreed targets are achieved.

In the longer term a new body called Great British Railways is planned to take over the running of the railways and specifically take over Network Rail's responsibilities as well as some functions currently carried out by the Department for Transport and Rail Delivery Group. The franchise model will be changed to one of concessions, although this will take some years to fully implement.

In London and on Merseyside concessions were already in place. These see the operator paid a fee to run the service, within tightly specified guidelines. Operators running a concession would not normally take commercial risks, although there are usually penalties and rewards in the contract.

Britain's national railway infrastructure is owned by a "not for dividend" company, Network Rail. In 2014 Network Rail was reclassified as a public sector company, being described by the Government as a "public sector arm's-length body of the Department for Transport".

Most stations and maintenance depots are leased to and operated by the Train Operating Companies (TOCs), but some larger stations are controlled by Network Rail. The only exception is the infrastructure on the Isle of Wight: The Island Line franchise uniquely included maintenance of the infrastructure as well as the operation of passenger services. Both the infrastructure and trains are operated by South Western Railway.

Trains are operated by TOCs over Network Rail tracks (termed the National Network), regulated by access agreements between the parties involved. In general, TOCs are responsible for the provision and maintenance of the trains and staff necessary for the direct operation of services, whilst

Network Rail is responsible for the provision and maintenance of the infrastructure and also for staff to regulate the operation of services.

The Department for Transport (DfT) is the authority for the national network. Transport Scotland has operated ScotRail since April 2022 and is also responsible for the Caledonian Sleeper franchises. In February 2021 the Welsh Government took over the operation of the Wales & Borders franchise (Transport for Wales) from KeolisAmey.

Each franchise was set up with the right to run specified services within a specified area for a period of time, in return for the right to charge fares and, where appropriate, to receive financial support from the Government. Subsidy was payable in respect of socially necessary services. Service standards are monitored by the DfT throughout the duration of the franchise. Franchisees earned revenue primarily from fares and from subsidy. They generally leased stations from Network Rail and earned rental income by sub-letting parts of them, for example to retailers.

TOC's and open access operator's main costs are the track access charges they pay to Network Rail, the costs of leasing stations and rolling stock and of employing staff. Franchisees may do light maintenance work on rolling stock or contract it out to other companies. Heavy maintenance is normally carried out by the Rolling Stock Leasing Companies, according to contracts.

DOMESTIC PASSENGER TRAIN OPERATORS

The majority of passenger trains are operated by Train Operating Companies, now supported by the Government through National Rail Contracts. For reference the date of the expiry of the original franchise is also given here (if later than the current NRC expiry date).

Name of franchise	Operator	Trading Name
Caledonian Sleeper	Scottish Government	**Caledonian Sleeper**
Operated by the Scottish Government		
Chiltern	Arriva (Deutsche Bahn)	**Chiltern Railways**
NRC until 1 April 2025 with the option to extend to December 2027		
Cross Country	Arriva (Deutsche Bahn)	**CrossCountry**
ERMA until 15 October 2027 with the option to extend to October 2031		
Crossrail	MTR	**Elizabeth Line**
Concession until 27 May 2025		
East Coast	DfT	**London North Eastern Railway**
Operated by DfT's "Operator of Last Resort" until June 2025		
East Midlands	Transport UK Group	**East Midlands Railway**
NRC until 17 October 2026 with the option to extend to October 2030		

East Anglia   Transport UK Group (60%)/Mitsui Group (40%)   **Greater Anglia**
NRC until 19 September 2024 with option for a 2 year extension; original franchise was until 11 October 2025

Essex Thameside   Trenitalia   **c2c**
NRC until 25 July 2025; original franchise was until 10 November 2029

Great Western   First Group   **Great Western Railway**
NRC until 21 June 2025 with the option to extend to June 2028

London Rail   Arriva (Deutsche Bahn)   **London Overground**
Concession until 3 May 2026

Merseyrail Electrics   Serco (50%)/Transport UK Group (50%)   **Merseyrail**
Concession until 22 July 2028. Under the control of Merseytravel PTE instead of the DfT
Due to be reviewed every five years to fit in with the Merseyside Local Transport Plan

Northern   DfT   **Northern**
Operated by DfT's "Operator of Last Resort" until further notice

ScotRail   Scottish Government   **ScotRail**
Operated by the Scottish Government from April 2022, having taken over ScotRail from Abellio

South Eastern   DfT   **Southeastern**
Operated by DfT's "Operator of Last Resort" until further notice.

South Western   First Group (70%)/MTR (30%)   **South Western Railway**
NRC until 25 May 2025

Thameslink, Southern &   Govia (Go-Ahead/Keolis)   **Govia Thameslink Railway**
Great Northern (TSGN)
NRC until 1 April 2025 with the option to extend to April 2028

Trans-Pennine Express   DfT   **TransPennine Express**
Operated by DfT's "Operator of Last Resort" until further notice.

Wales & Borders   Welsh Government   **Transport for Wales**
From February 2021 the Welsh Government took direct control of rail service operation.
Infrastructure management continues to be managed by KeolisAmey.

West Coast Partnership   First Group (70%)/Trenitalia (30%)   **Avanti West Coast**
NRC until 18 October 2026 with the option to extend to October 2032

West Midlands Trains   Transport UK Group (70%)/JR East (15%)/ **West Midlands Railway/**
Mitsui (15%)   **London Northwestern**
NRC until 19 September 2024 with option to extend to September 2026; original franchise ran until 31 March 2026

NON-FRANCHISED SERVICES

The following operators run non-franchised, or "open access" services (* special seasonal services):

Operator	Trading Name	Route
Heathrow Airport Holdings	Heathrow Express	London Paddington–Heathrow Airport
Hull Trains (part of First)	Hull Trains	London King's Cross–Hull
Grand Central (part of Arriva)	Grand Central	London King's Cross–Sunderland/Bradford Interchange
Locomotive Services (TOC)	Locomotive Services	
First East Coast	Lumo	London King's Cross–Edinburgh
North Yorkshire Moors Railway Enterprises	North Yorkshire Moors Railway	Pickering–Grosmont–Whitby/Sheringham–Cromer*
South Yorkshire Supertram	Stagecoach Supertram	Meadowhall South–Rotherham Parkgate
Tyne & Wear PTE	Tyne & Wear Metro	Pelaw–Sunderland
Vintage Trains	Vintage Trains	Birmingham Snow Hill–Stratford-upon-Avon*
West Coast Railway Company	West Coast Railway Company	Fort William–Mallaig* York–Settle–Carlisle* Carnforth–York–Scarborough*

INTERNATIONAL PASSENGER OPERATORS

Eurostar International operates passenger services between London St Pancras and mainland Europe. The company, established in 2010, is jointly owned by SNCF (the national operator of France): 55%, SNCB (the national operator of Belgium): 5% and Patina Rail: 40%. Patina Rail is made up of Canadian-based Caisse de dépôt et placement du Québec (CDPG) and UK-based Hermes Infrastructure (owning 30% and 10% respectively). This 40% was previously owned by the UK Government until it was sold in 2015.

In addition, a service for the conveyance of accompanied road vehicles through the Channel Tunnel is provided by the tunnel operating company, Eurotunnel. All Eurotunnel services are operated in top-and-tail mode by the powerful Class 9 Bo-Bo-Bo locomotives.

INTRODUCTION

This book contains details of all Diesel Multiple Units, usually referred to as DMUs, which can run on Britain's national railway network.

Since the 1980s DMUs have replaced more traditional locomotive-hauled trains on many routes. DMUs today work a wide variety of services, from long distance Intercity to inter-urban and suburban duties.

LAYOUT OF INFORMATION

DMUs are listed in numerical order of set – using current numbers as allocated by the Rolling Stock Library. Individual "loose" vehicles are listed in numerical order after vehicles formed into fixed formations. Where sets or vehicles have been renumbered in recent years, former numbering detail is shown in parentheses. Each entry is laid out as in the following example:

RSL Set No.	Detail	Livery	Owner	Operator	Depot	Formation	
156 505	w	**SR**	A	*SR*	CK	52505	57505

Codes: Codes are used to denote the livery, owner, operator and depot allocation of each Diesel Multiple Unit. Details of these can be found in section 5 of this book. Where a unit or spare car is off-lease, the operator column is left blank.

Detail Differences: Detail differences which currently affect the areas and types of train which vehicles may work are shown, plus differences in interior layout. Where such differences occur within a class, these are shown either in the heading information or alongside the individual set or vehicle number. The following standard abbreviations are used:

e   European Railway Traffic Management System (ERTMS) signalling equipment fitted.
r   Radio Electric Token Block signalling equipment fitted.

Use of the above abbreviations indicates the equipment fitted is normally operable. Meaning of non-standard abbreviations is detailed in individual class headings.

Set Formations: Regular set formations are shown where these are normally maintained. Readers should note set formations might be temporarily varied from time to time to suit maintenance and/or operational requirements. Vehicles shown as "Spare" are not formed in any regular set formation.

Names: Only names carried with official sanction are listed. Names are shown in UPPER/lower case characters as actually shown on the name carried on the vehicle(s). Unless otherwise shown, complete units are regarded as named rather than just the individual car(s) which carry the name.

GENERAL INFORMATION

CLASSIFICATION AND NUMBERING

DMU Classes are listed in class number order.

First generation ("Heritage") DMUs were classified in the series 100–139.
Parry People Movers (not technically DMUs) are classified in the series 139.
Second generation DMUs are classified in the series 140–199.
Diesel Electric Multiple Units are classified in the series 200–249.
Service units are classified in the series 930–999.

First and second generation individual cars are numbered in the series 50000–59999 and 79000–79999.

Parry People Mover cars are numbered in the 39000 series.

DEMU individual cars are numbered in the series 60000–60999, except for a few former EMU vehicles which retain their EMU numbers.

For all new vehicles allocated by the Rolling Stock Library since 2014 6-digit vehicle numbers are being used. The Class 230 D-Train DEMU or battery unit individual cars are numbered in the 300xxx series.

WHEEL ARRANGEMENT

A system whereby the number of powered axles on a bogie or frame is denoted by a letter (A = 1, B = 2, C= 3 etc) and the number of unpowered axles is denoted by a number is used in this publication. The letter "o" after a letter indicates that each axle is individually powered.

UNITS OF MEASUREMENT

Principal details and dimensions are quoted for each class in metric and/or imperial units as considered appropriate bearing in mind common UK usage.

All dimensions and weights are quoted for vehicles in an "as new" condition with all necessary supplies (eg oil, water, sand) on board. Dimensions are quoted in the order Length – Width. All lengths quoted are over buffers or couplers as appropriate. Where two lengths are quoted, the first refers to outer vehicles in a set and the second to inner vehicles. All width dimensions quoted are maxima. All weights are shown as metric tonnes (t = tonnes).

OPERATING CODES

These codes are used by railway operating staff to describe the various different types of vehicles and normally appear on data panels on the inner (ie non driving) ends of vehicles.

The first part of the code describes whether the car has a motor or a driving cab as follows:

DM Driving motor   DT Driving trailer   M   Motor   T   Trailer

The next letter is a "B" for cars with a brake compartment.
This is followed by the saloon details:

F	First	L	denotes a vehicle with a toilet.
S	Standard	W	denotes a Wheelchair space.
C	Composite		

Finally vehicles with a buffet or kitchen area are suffixed RB or RMB for a miniature buffet counter.

Where two vehicles of the same type are formed within the same unit, the above codes may be suffixed by (A) and (B) to differentiate between the vehicles.

A composite is a vehicle containing both First and Standard Class accommodation, whilst a brake vehicle is a vehicle containing separate specific accommodation for the conductor.

Where vehicles have been declassified, the correct operating code which describes the actual vehicle layout is quoted in this publication.

BUILD DETAILS

Lot Numbers

Vehicles ordered under the auspices of BR were allocated a Lot (batch) number when ordered and these are quoted in class headings and sub-headings. Vehicles ordered since 1995 have no Lot Numbers, but the manufacturer and location that they were built is given.

ACCOMMODATION

The information given in class headings and sub-headings is in the form F/S nT (or TD) nW. For example, 12/54 1T 1W denotes 12 First Class and 54 Standard Class seats, one toilet and one space for a wheelchair. A number in brackets (ie (+2)) denotes tip-up seats (in addition to the fixed seats). The seating layout of open saloons is indicated as 2+1, 2+2 or 3+2. Where units have First Class accommodation as well as Standard Class and the layout is different for each class then these are shown separately prefixed by "1:" and "2:".

TD denotes a universal access toilet suitable for use by people with disabilities. By law all trains should have been fitted with such facilities by the start of 2020. All serviceable DMUs have now been fitted with a universal access toilet apart from a handful of Transport for Wales Class 153/9s which must operate with a PRM compliant unit and have had their toilets locked out of use.

1. DIESEL MECHANICAL & DIESEL HYDRAULIC UNITS

1.1. FIRST GENERATION UNITS

CLASS 117   PRESSED STEEL SUBURBAN

First generation 3-car unit registered for use on the Swanage Railway services into Wareham station only. No set number is carried.
Construction: Steel.
Engines: Two Leyland 680/1 of 112 kW (150 hp) at 1800 rpm.
Transmission: Mechanical. Cardan shaft and freewheel to a four-speed epicyclic gearbox and final drive.
Bogies: DD10 (motor) and DT9 (trailer).
Brakes: Vacuum.
Couplers: Screw.
Dimensions: 20.45 x 2.82 m.
Gangways: Within unit.
Doors: Manually-operated slam.
Maximum Speed: 70 mph.
Seating Layout: 3+2 facing.
Multiple Working: "Blue Square" coupling code. First Generation vehicles cannot be coupled to Second Generation units.

DMBS. Lot No. 30546 1959–60. –/65. 36.5 t.
TCL: Lot No. 30547 1959–60. 22/48 2T. 30.5 t.
DMS: Lot No. 30548 1959–60. –/89. 36.5 t.

| – | **G** | SG | *SG* | SW | 51356 | 59486 | 51388 |

CLASS 121   PRESSED STEEL SUBURBAN

First generation units.
Construction: Steel.
Engines: Two Leyland 1595 of 112 kW (150 hp) at 1800 rpm.
Transmission: Mechanical. Cardan shaft and freewheel to a four-speed epicyclic gearbox and final drive.
Bogies: DD10.
Brakes: Vacuum.
Couplers: Screw.
Dimensions: 20.45 x 2.82 m.
Gangways: Non gangwayed single cars with cabs at each end.
Wheel arrangement: 1-A + A-1.
Doors: Manually-operated slam.
Maximum Speed: 70 mph.
Seating Layout: 3+2 facing (121022 has a heavily modified interior).

Multiple Working: "Blue Square" coupling code. First Generation vehicles cannot be coupled to Second Generation units.

121022 was formerly in departmental use as 977873. Refurbished in 2023 as a Locomotive Services executive vehicle.

121028 was formerly registered in departmental use as 977860. Now registered for use on the Swanage Railway services into Wareham station only.

121034 was formerly in departmental use as 977828 and then used by Chiltern Railways until 2017. Currently on loan to the Ecclesbourne Valley Railway. Fitted with central door locking.

DMBS. Lot No. 30518 1960. –/65. 38.0 t.

121022	**CC**	LS	*LS*	CL	55022	FLORA
121028	**G**	SG	*SG*	SW	55028	
121034	**G**	LS	*LS*	CL	55034	

1.2. PARRY PEOPLE MOVERS

CLASS 139   PPM-60

Gas/flywheel hybrid drive Railcars used on the Stourbridge Junction–Stourbridge Town branch.
Body construction: Stainless steel framework.
Chassis construction: Welded mild steel box section.
Primary Drive: Ford MVH420 2.3 litre 64 kW (86 hp) LPG fuel engine driving through Newage marine gearbox, Tandler bevel box and 4 "V" belt driver to flywheel.
Flywheel Energy Store: 500 kg, 1 m diameter, normal operational speed range 1000–1500 rpm.
Final transmission: 4 "V" belt driver from flywheel to Tandler bevel box, Linde hydrostatic transmission and spiral bevel gearbox at No. 2 end axle.
Braking: Normal service braking by regeneration to flywheel (1 m/s/s); emergency/parking braking by sprung-on, air-off disc brakes (3 m/s/s).
Maximum Speed: 45 mph.   **Dimensions:** 8.7 x 2.4 m.
Doors: Deans powered doors, double-leaf folding (one per side).
Seating Layout: 1+1 unidirectional/facing.
Multiple Working: Not applicable.

39001–002. DMS. Main Road Sheet Metal, Leyland 2007–08. –/17(+4) 1W. 12.5 t.

139001	**WM**	P	*WM*	SJ	39001
139002	**WM**	P	*WM*	SJ	39002

1.3. SECOND GENERATION UNITS

All units in this section have air brakes and are equipped with public address, with transmission equipment on driving vehicles and flexible diaphragm gangways. Except where otherwise stated, transmission is Voith 211r hydraulic with a cardan shaft to a Gmeinder GM190 final drive.

CLASS 142   PACER   BREL DERBY/LEYLAND

DMS–DMSL. The remaining Class 142s were withdrawn from normal passenger service at the end of 2020 and most have now been disposed of, either for scrap or preservation. Some can be found in the DMUs in Industrial Service section (Section 3).

Construction: Steel underframe, rivetted steel body and roof. Built from Leyland National bus parts on Leyland Bus four-wheeled underframes.
Engines: One Cummins LT10-R of 165 kW (225 hp) at 1950 rpm.
Couplers: BSI at outer ends, bar within unit.
Dimensions: 15.55 x 2.80 m.

Gangways: Within unit only.	**Wheel Arrangement:** 1-A + A-1.
Doors: Twin-leaf inward pivoting.	**Maximum Speed:** 75 mph.

Seating Layout: 3+2 mainly unidirectional bus/bench style unless stated.
Multiple Working: Within class and with Classes 143, 144, 150, 153, 155, 156, 158 and 159.

Non-standard liveries:

142 003 Original Greater Manchester PTE (orange & brown).
142 013 Revised Greater Manchester PTE (light grey/dark grey with red & white stripes).

t   Former First North Western facelifted units – DMS fitted with a luggage/ bicycle rack and wheelchair space.

55544–588. DMS. Lot No. 31003 1985–86. –/62 (t –/53 or 55 1W). 24.5 t.
55594–638. DMSL. Lot No. 31004 1985–86. –/59 1T. 25.0 t.

142 003		**0**	LS	*LS*	CL	55544	55594
142 007	t	**0**	LS	*LS*	CL	55548	55598
142 014	t	**N0**	LS		ZG	55555	55605
Spare		**N0**	A		GA	55588	(ex-142 047)

CLASS 144   PACER   ALEXANDER/BREL DERBY

DMS–DMSL or DMS–MS–DMSL. As Class 143, but underframes built by BREL. Class 144s finished in service with Northern in 2020. Many have since been preserved or can be found in DMUs in Industrial Service (Section 3).

Construction: Steel underframe, aluminium alloy body and roof. Alexander bus bodywork on four-wheeled underframes.
Engines: One Cummins LT10-R of 165 kW (225 hp) at 1950 rpm.
Couplers: BSI at outer ends, bar within unit.
Dimensions: 15.45/15.43 x 2.80 m.

Gangways: Within unit only.   **Wheel Arrangement:** 1-A + A-1.
Doors: Twin-leaf inward pivoting.   **Maximum Speed:** 75 mph.
Seating Layout: 2+2 high-back Richmond seating, mainly unidirectional.
Multiple Working: Within class and with Classes 142, 143, 150, 153, 155, 156, 158 and 159.

DMS. Lot No. 31015 BREL Derby 1986–87. –/45(+3) 1W 24.0 t.
MS. Lot No. 31037 BREL Derby 1987. –/58. 23.5 t.
DMSL. Lot No. 31016 BREL Derby 1986–87. –/41(+3) 1T. 24.5 t.

144 005	**NO**	LO	WS	55805		55828	
144 019	**NO**	VT	TM	55819	55855	55842	
Spare	**NO**	VT	TM	55850			(ex-144 014)
Spare	**NO**	VT	TM	55859	55846		(ex-144 023)

CLASS 150/0   PROTOTYPE SPRINTER BREL YORK

DMSL–MS–DMS. Prototype Sprinter.

Construction: Steel.
Engines: One Cummins NT855R5 of 213 kW (285 hp) at 2100 rpm.
Bogies: BX8P (powered), BX8T (non-powered).
Couplers: BSI at outer end of driving vehicles, bar non-driving ends.
Dimensions: 19.93/19.92 x 2.73 m.
Gangways: Within unit only.   **Wheel Arrangement:** 2-B + 2-B + B-2.
Doors: Twin-leaf sliding.   **Maximum Speed:** 75 mph.
Seating Layout: 3+2 (mainly unidirectional).
Multiple Working: Within class and with Classes 142, 143, 144, 153, 155, 156, 158, 159, 170 and 172.

DMSL. Lot No. 30984 1984. –/58(+3) 1TD 2W. 35.4 t.
MS. Lot No. 30986 1984. –/91. 38.2 t.
DMS. Lot No. 30985 1984. –/69(+6). 36.1 t.

| 150 001 | **NR** | A | *NO* | NL | 55200 | 55400 | 55300 |
| 150 002 | **NR** | A | *NO* | NL | 55201 | 55401 | 55301 |

CLASS 150/0   SPRINTER   BREL YORK

DMSL–DMS–DMS (150 005 DMSL–DMSL–DMS). In 2021 Northern reformed 150 003–006 as new 3-car units using a 150/1 unit with a 150/2 vehicle inserted as a centre car.

Construction: Steel.
Engines: One Cummins NT855R5 of 213 kW (285 hp) at 2100 rpm.
Bogies: BP38 (powered), BT38 (non-powered).
Couplers: BSI.   **Dimensions:** 19.74 x 2.82 m.
Gangways: Within unit only.
Wheel Arrangement: 2-B + 2-B/B-2 + B-2.
Doors: Twin-leaf sliding.   **Maximum Speed:** 75 mph.

Seating Layout: 3+2 facing/unidirectional.
Multiple Working: Within class and with Classes 142, 143, 144, 153, 155, 156, 158, 159, 170 and 172.

DMSL. Lot No. 31011 1985–86. † –/56(+3) 1TD 2W, * –/55(+3) 1TD 2W. 38.3 t.
DMS. Lot No. 31018 1986–87. † –/70(+6), * –/58(+10). 36.5 t.
DMSL (52223). Lot No. 31017 1986–87. –/58(+3) 1TD 2W. 37.5 t.
DMS. Lot No. 31012 1985–86. † –/70(+6), * –/65. 38.1 t.

150 003	†	**NR**	A	*NO*	NL	52116	57209	57116
150 004	†	**NR**	A	*NO*	NL	52112	57212	57112
150 005	†	**NR**	A	*NO*	NL	52117	52223	57117
150 006	*	**NR**	A	*NO*	NL	52147	57223	57147

CLASS 150/1   SPRINTER   BREL YORK

DMSL–DMS.

Construction: Steel.
Engines: One Cummins NT855R5 of 213 kW (285 hp) at 2100 rpm.
Bogies: BP38 (powered), BT38 (non-powered).
Couplers: BSI.   **Dimensions:** 19.74 x 2.82 m.
Gangways: Within unit only.   **Wheel Arrangement:** 2-B + B-2.
Doors: Twin-leaf sliding.   **Maximum Speed:** 75 mph.
Seating Layout: 3+2 facing as built but units operated by Centro were reseated with mainly unidirectional seating.
Multiple Working: Within class and with Classes 142, 143, 144, 153, 155, 156, 158, 159, 170 and 172.

† Refurbished Northern units with original Ashbourne seating.
* Refurbished Northern or LNR units. Chapman seating.

DMSL. Lot No. 31011 1985–86. † –/56(+3) or 58(+3) 1TD 2W, * –/55(+3) 1TD 2W. 38.3 t.
DMS. Lot No. 31012 1985–86. † –/70(+6) or –/71(+6)), * –/65. 38.1 t.

150 101	†	**NR**	A	*NO*	NH	52101	57101
150 102	†	**NR**	A	*NO*	NH	52102	57102
150 103	†	**NR**	A	*NO*	NH	52103	57103
150 104	†	**NR**	A	*NO*	NH	52104	57104
150 105	†	**NR**	A	*NO*	NH	52105	57105
150 106	†	**NR**	A	*NO*	NH	52106	57106
150 107	†	**NR**	A	*NO*	NH	52107	57107
150 108	†	**NR**	A	*NO*	NH	52108	57108
150 109	†	**NR**	A	*NO*	NH	52109	57109
150 110	†	**NR**	A	*NO*	NH	52110	57110
150 111	†	**NR**	A	*NO*	NH	52111	57111
150 113	†	**NR**	A	*NO*	NH	52113	57113
150 114	†	**NR**	A	*NO*	NH	52114	57114
150 115	†	**NR**	A	*NO*	NH	52115	57115
150 118	†	**NR**	A	*NO*	NH	52118	57118
150 119	†	**NR**	A	*NO*	NH	52119	57119
150 120	†	**NR**	A	*NO*	NH	52120	57120

150 121	†	**NR**	A	*NO*	NH	52121	57121
150 122	†	**NR**	A	*NO*	NH	52122	57122
150 123	†	**NR**	A	*NO*	NH	52123	57123
150 124	†	**NR**	A	*NO*	NH	52124	57124
150 125	†	**NR**	A	*NO*	NH	52125	57125
150 126	†	**NR**	A	*NO*	NH	52126	57126
150 127	†	**NR**	A	*NO*	NH	52127	57127
150 128	†	**NR**	A	*NO*	NH	52128	57128
150 129	†	**NR**	A	*NO*	NH	52129	57129
150 130	†	**NR**	A	*NO*	NH	52130	57130
150 131	†	**NR**	A	*NO*	NH	52131	57131
150 132	†	**NR**	A	*NO*	NH	52132	57132
150 133	*	**NR**	A	*NO*	NH	52133	57133
150 134	*	**NR**	A	*NO*	NH	52134	57134
150 135	*	**NR**	A	*NO*	NH	52135	57135
150 136	*	**NR**	A	*NO*	NH	52136	57136
150 137	*	**LN**	A	*WM*	BY	52137	57137
150 138	*	**NR**	A	*NO*	NH	52138	57138
150 139	*	**LN**	A	*WM*	BY	52139	57139
150 140	*	**NR**	A	*NO*	NH	52140	57140
150 141	*	**LN**	A	*WM*	BY	52141	57141
150 142	*	**NR**	A	*NO*	NH	52142	57142
150 143	*	**NR**	A	*NO*	NH	52143	57143
150 144	*	**NR**	A	*NO*	NH	52144	57144
150 145	*	**NR**	A	*NO*	NH	52145	57145
150 146	*	**NR**	A	*NO*	NH	52146	57146
150 148	*	**NR**	A	*NO*	NH	52148	57148
150 149	*	**NR**	A	*NO*	NH	52149	57149
150 150	*	**NR**	A	*NO*	NH	52150	57150

CLASS 150/2   SPRINTER   BREL YORK

DMSL–DMS.

Construction: Steel.
Engines: One Cummins NT855R5 of 213 kW (285 hp) at 2100 rpm.
Bogies: BP38 (powered), BT38 (non-powered).
Couplers: BSI.   **Dimensions:** 19.74 x 2.82 m.
Gangways: Throughout.   **Wheel Arrangement:** 2-B + B-2.
Doors: Twin-leaf sliding.   **Maximum Speed:** 75 mph.
Seating Layout: 3+2 mainly unidirectional seating as built, but most units have now been refurbished with new 2+2 seating.
Multiple Working: Within class and with Classes 142, 143, 144, 153, 155, 156, 158, 159, 170 and 172.

c   Former First North Western units with 3+2 Chapman seating.
q   Refurbished Great Western Railway units. Original Ashbourne seating. Full details awaited.
t   Refurbished Transport for Wales units with 2+2 Chapman seating.
*   Refurbished Great Western Railway units with 2+2 Chapman seating.
†   Refurbished Northern units. 3+2 Chapman seating.

§ Refurbished Northern units. Original Ashbourne seating.

150 269 and 150 270 are on sub-lease from Northern to TfW.

DMSL. Lot No. 31017 1986–87. * –/50(+4) 1TD 2W, † –/58(+3) 1TD 2W,
§ –/58(+3) 1TD 2W, c –/62 1TD, t –/50 1TD 2W. 37.5 t (* 35.8 t, † and § 38.1 t).
DMS. Lot No. 31018 1986–87. * –/58(+10), † –/70(+6), § –/72(+3), c –/70,
t –/58(+4). 36.5 t.

150 201	†	**NR**	A	*NO*	NL	52201 57201
150 202	q	**GW**	A	*GW*	EX	52202 57202
150 203	†	**NR**	A	*NO*	NL	52203 57203
150 204	†	**NR**	A	*NO*	NL	52204 57204
150 205	†	**NR**	A	*NO*	NL	52205 57205
150 206	†	**NR**	A	*NO*	NL	52206 57206
150 207	c	**GW**	A	*NO*	EX	52207 57207
150 208	t	**TW**	P	*TW*	CF	52208 57208
150 210	†	**NR**	A	*NO*	NL	52210 57210
150 211	†	**NR**	A	*NO*	NL	52211 57211
150 213	t	**TW**	P	*TW*	CF	52213 57213
150 214	§	**NR**	A	*NO*	NL	52214 57214
150 215	†	**NR**	A	*NO*	NL	52215 57215
150 216	q	**GW**	A	*GW*	EX	52216 57216
150 217	t	**TW**	P	*TW*	CF	52217 57217
150 218	†	**NR**	A	*NO*	NL	52218 57218
150 219	*	**FB**	P	*GW*	EX	52219 57219
150 220	§	**NR**	A	*NO*	NL	52220 57220
150 221	*	**GW**	P	*GW*	EX	52221 57221
150 222	†	**NR**	A	*NO*	NL	52222 57222
150 224	†	**NR**	A	*NO*	NH	52224 57224
150 225	†	**NR**	A	*NO*	NH	52225 57225
150 226	†	**NR**	A	*NO*	NH	52226 57226
150 227	t	**TW**	P	*TW*	CF	52227 57227
150 228	§	**NR**	P	*NO*	NL	52228 57228
150 229	t	**TW**	P	*TW*	CF	52229 57229
150 230	t	**TW**	P	*TW*	CF	52230 57230
150 231	t	**TW**	P	*TW*	CF	52231 57231
150 232	*	**GW**	P	*GW*	EX	52232 57232
150 233	*	**GW**	P	*GW*	EX	52233 57233
150 234	*	**GW**	P	*GW*	EX	52234 57234
150 235	t	**TW**	P	*TW*	CF	52235 57235
150 236	t	**TW**	P	*TW*	CF	52236 57236
150 237	t	**TW**	P	*TW*	CF	52237 57237
150 238	*	**FB**	P	*GW*	EX	52238 57238
150 239	*	**GW**	P	*GW*	EX	52239 57239
150 240	t	**TW**	P	*TW*	CF	52240 57240
150 241	t	**TW**	P	*TW*	CF	52241 57241
150 242	t	**TW**	P	*TW*	CF	52242 57242
150 243	*	**GW**	P	*GW*	EX	52243 57243
150 244	*	**GW**	P	*GW*	EX	52244 57244
150 245	t	**TW**	P	*TW*	CF	52245 57245
150 246	*	**GW**	P	*GW*	EX	52246 57246

150 247	*	**GW**	P	*GW*	EX	52247	57247
150 248	*	**GW**	P	*GW*	EX	52248	57248
150 249	*	**GW**	P	*GW*	EX	52249	57249
150 250	t	**TW**	P	*TW*	CF	52250	57250
150 251	t	**TW**	P	*TW*	CF	52251	57251
150 252	t	**TW**	P	*TW*	CF	52252	57252
150 253	t	**TW**	P	*TW*	CF	52253	57253
150 254	t	**TW**	P	*TW*	CF	52254	57254
150 255	t	**TW**	P	*TW*	CF	52255	57255
150 256	t	**TW**	P	*TW*	CF	52256	57256
150 257	t	**TW**	P	*TW*	CF	52257	57257
150 258	t	**TW**	P	*TW*	CF	52258	57258
150 259	t	**TW**	P	*TW*	CF	52259	57259
150 260	t	**TW**	P	*TW*	CF	52260	57260
150 261	*	**GW**	P	*GW*	EX	52261	57261
150 262	t	**TW**	P	*TW*	CF	52262	57262
150 263	*	**GW**	P	*GW*	EX	52263	57263
150 264	t	**TW**	P	*TW*	CF	52264	57264
150 265	*	**GW**	P	*GW*	EX	52265	57265
150 266	*	**GW**	P	*GW*	EX	52266	57266
150 267	t	**TW**	P	*TW*	CF	52267	57267
150 268	§	**NR**	P	*NO*	NL	52268	57268
150 269	§	**NR**	P	*TW*	CF	52269	57269
150 270	§	**NR**	P	*TW*	CF	52270	57270
150 271	§	**NR**	P	*NO*	NL	52271	57271
150 272	§	**NR**	P	*NO*	NL	52272	57272
150 273	§	**NR**	P	*NO*	NL	52273	57273
150 274	§	**NR**	P	*NO*	NL	52274	57274
150 275	§	**NR**	P	*NO*	NL	52275	57275
150 276	§	**NR**	P	*NO*	NL	52276	57276
150 277	§	**NR**	P	*NO*	NL	52277	57277
150 278	t	**TW**	P	*TW*	CF	52278	57278
150 279	t	**AW**	P	*TW*	CF	52279	57279
150 280	t	**TW**	P	*TW*	CF	52280	57280
150 281	t	**TW**	P	*TW*	CF	52281	57281
150 282	t	**TW**	P	*TW*	CF	52282	57282
150 283	t	**TW**	P	*TW*	CF	52283	57283
150 284	t	**TW**	P	*TW*	CF	52284	57284
150 285	t	**TW**	P	*TW*	CF	52285	57285

Names:

150 214	The Bentham Line A Dementia-Friendly Railway
150 233	Peter West OBE
150 275	The Yorkshire Regiment Yorkshire Warrior

CLASS 153   SUPER SPRINTER   LEYLAND BUS

DMSL. Converted by Hunslet-Barclay, Kilmarnock from Class 155 2-car units. The only Class 153s remaining in passenger service now are with Transport for Wales and ScotRail.

Construction: Steel underframe, rivetted steel body and roof. Built from Leyland National bus parts on Leyland Bus bogied underframes.
Engine: One Cummins NT855R5 of 213 kW (285 hp) at 2100 rpm.
Bogies: One P3-10 (powered) and one BT38 (non-powered).
Couplers: BSI.
Dimensions: 23.21 x 2.70 m.

Gangways: Throughout.	**Wheel Arrangement:** 2-B.
Doors: Single-leaf sliding plug.	**Maximum Speed:** 75 mph.

Seating Layout: 2+2 facing/unidirectional.
Multiple Working: Within class and with Classes 142, 143, 144, 150, 155, 156, 158, 159, 170 and 172.

Cars numbered in the 573xx series were renumbered by adding 50 to their original number so that the last two digits correspond with the set number.
c   Chapman seating.
d   Richmond seating.
†   Refurbished Transport for Wales units with a new universal access toilet.

§   153305/370/373/377/380 have been converted to "active travel" bicycle carrying vehicles by ScotRail for West Highland Line services. Richmond seating.
n   These units now form part of the Network Rail infrastructure monitoring or testing fleet and have been fitted with additional equipment such as for switch & crossing monitoring.

Non-standard liveries:

153305/370/373/377/380 ScotRail active travel (**SR** livery with various graphics).
153317   Light grey
153376   Light blue

52301–52335. DMSL. Lot No. 31026 1987–88. Converted under Lot No. 31115 1991–92. –/72(+3) 1T 1W. (s –/72 1T 1W, t –/72(+2) 1T 1W), † –/56(+5) 1TD 2W, § –/24 1T + bike/luggage racks). 41.2 t.
57301–57335. DMSL. Lot No. 31027 1987–88. Converted under Lot No. 31115 1991–92. –/72(+3) 1T 1W. (s –/72 1T 1W, † –/56(+5) 1TD 2W, § –/24 1T + bike/luggage racks). 41.2 t.

153 301	d	**NO**	A		EP	52301
153 303	†c	**TW**	TW	*TW*	CF	52303
153 304	ds	**NO**	A		EP	52304
153 305	§	**0**	A	*SR*	CK	52305
153 308	c	**EM**	A		EP	52308
153 311	n	**EM**	P	*CS*	ZA	52311
153 312	†	**TW**	TW	*TW*	CF	52312
153 315	ds	**NO**	A		EP	52315
153 317	n	**0**	A		BQ	52317
153 318	d	**TW**	TW	*TW*	CF	52318

153 319	c	**EM**	A		EP	52319	
153 320	†c	**TW**	P	*TW*	CF	52320	
153 323	†c	**TW**	P	*TW*	CF	52323	
153 325	†c	**TW**	P	*TW*	CF	52325	
153 327	†c	**TW**	TW	*TW*	CF	52327	
153 329	†c	**TW**	P	*TW*	CF	52329	
153 330	cs	**NO**	P		LM	52330	
153 332	c	**NO**	P		LM	52332	
153 333	†c	**TW**	P	*TW*	CF	52333	
153 334	ct	**LM**	P		LM	52334	
153 351	d	**NO**	A		EP	57351	
153 353	†c	**TW**	TW	*TW*	CF	57353	
153 354	c	**LM**	P		LM	57354	
153 355	c	**EM**	A		EP	57355	
153 356	c	**LM**	P		LM	57356	
153 357	c	**EM**	A		EP	57357	
153 358	c	**NO**	P		LM	57358	
153 360	c	**NO**	P		LM	57360	
153 361	†c	**TW**	P	*TW*	CF	57361	
153 362	†c	**TW**	TW	*TW*	CF	57362	
153 363	cs	**NO**	P		LM	57363	
153 365	c	**LM**	P		LM	57365	
153 367	†c	**TW**	P	*TW*	CF	57367	
153 369	†c	**TW**	P	*TW*	CF	57369	
153 370	§	**0**	A	*SR*	CK	57370	
153 371	c	**LM**	P		LM	57371	
153 373	§	**0**	A	*SR*	CK	57373	
153 375	c	**LM**	P		LM	57375	
153 376	n	**0**	P	*CS*	ZA	57376	
153 377	§	**0**	A	*SR*	CK	57377	
153 378	d	**NO**	A		EP	57378	
153 379	n	**EM**	P	*CS*	ZA	57379	
153 380	§	**0**	A	*SR*	CK	57380	
153 381	c	**EM**	P		LM	57381	
153 382	d	**TW**	TW	*TW*	CF	57382	
153 383	c	**EM**	P		LM	57383	Ecclesbourne Valley Railway 150 Years
153 384	n	**EM**	P	*CS*	ZA	57384	
153 385	n	**EM**	P	*CS*	ZA	57385	

Class 153/5. Transport for Wales units being rebuilt or to be rebuilt as "active travel" units with additional space for bicycles. 153 568 and 153 572 will be renumbered from 153/9s. Full details awaited.

153 507	(153 307)	**NO**	TW	LE	52307
153 528	(153 328)	**NO**	TW	LE	52328
153 531	(153 331)	**NO**	TW	LE	52331
153 552	(153 352)	**NO**	TW	LE	57352
153 568	(153 968)				
153 572	(153 972)				

Class 153/9. Transport for Wales units that are not fully PRM compliant. Renumbered into the 1539xx series as they should operate with a PRM compliant unit. Toilets locked out of use.

153 906	(153306)	c	**TW**	P	*TW*	CF	52306
153 909	(153309)	c	**TW**	P	*TW*	CF	52309
153 910	(153310)	c	**TW**	P	*TW*	CF	52310
153 913	(153313)	cs	**TW**	P	*TW*	CF	52313
153 914	(153314)	c	**TW**	P	*TW*	CF	52314
153 921	(153321)	ct	**TW**	P	*TW*	CF	52321
153 922	(153322)	c	**TW**	P	*TW*	CF	52322
153 926	(153326)	c	**TW**	P	*TW*	CF	52326
153 935	(153335)	c	**TW**	P	*TW*	CF	52335
153 968	(153368)	d	**TW**	TW	*TW*	CF	57368
153 972	(153372)	d	**TW**	TW	*TW*	CF	57372

CLASS 155   SUPER SPRINTER   LEYLAND BUS

DMSL–DMS. Fitted with a universal access toilet.

Construction: Steel underframe, rivetted steel body and roof. Built from Leyland National bus parts on Leyland Bus bogied underframes.
Engines: One Cummins NT855R5 of 213 kW (285 hp) at 2100 rpm.
Bogies: One P3-10 (powered) and one BT38 (non-powered).
Couplers: BSI.
Dimensions: 23.21 x 2.70 m.
Gangways: Throughout.   **Wheel Arrangement:** 2-B + B-2.
Doors: Single-leaf sliding plug.   **Maximum Speed:** 75 mph.
Seating Layout: 2+2 facing/unidirectional Chapman seating.
Multiple Working: Within class and with Classes 142, 143, 144, 150, 153, 156, 158, 159, 170 and 172.
DMSL. Lot No. 31057 1988. –/64 1TD 2W. 39.0 t.
DMS. Lot No. 31058 1988. –/76. 40.4 t.

155 341	**NR**	P	*NO*	NL	52341	57341
155 342	**NR**	P	*NO*	NL	52342	57342
155 343	**NR**	P	*NO*	NL	52343	57343
155 344	**NR**	P	*NO*	NL	52344	57344
155 345	**NR**	P	*NO*	NL	52345	57345
155 346	**NR**	P	*NO*	NL	52346	57346
155 347	**NR**	P	*NO*	NL	52347	57347

CLASS 156   SUPER SPRINTER   METRO-CAMMELL

DMSL–DMS.

Construction: Steel.
Engines: One Cummins NT855R5 of 213 kW (285 hp) at 2100 rpm.
Bogies: One P3-10 (powered) and one BT38 (non-powered).
Couplers: BSI.
Dimensions: 23.03 x 2.73 m.
Gangways: Throughout.   **Wheel Arrangement:** 2-B + B-2.
Doors: Single-leaf sliding.   **Maximum Speed:** 75 mph.
Seating Layout: 2+2 facing/unidirectional.
Multiple Working: Within class and with Classes 142, 143, 144, 150, 153, 155, 158, 159, 170 and 172.

† Former Greater Anglia units. Chapman seating.
* Angel-owned Northern units. Richmond seating.
§ Porterbrook-owned Northern units. Chapman seating.
b Refurbished by Brodies, Kilmarnock with Fainsa seating.
m Northern units (ex-East Midlands Railway). Chapman seating.
n Northern units refurbished with new Fainsa seating.
w ScotRail units refurbished with new Fainsa seating.

156402/409/412/416–418/419/422 were renumbered 156902/909/912/916–918/919/922 respectively for a time during 2019–22.

Northern promotional vinyls: 156480 Royal Air Force (light blue & white)

DMSL. Lot No. 31028 1987–89. † –/62 1TD 2W, * –/64(+2) 1TD 2W, § –/62(+2) 1TD 2W, n –/66 1TD 2W, m –/62 (+2) 1TD 2W, u –/68, w –/66(+3) 1TD 2W. 38.6 t.
DMS. Lot No. 31029 1987–89. † and n –/74, *–/72(+4), u –/72, w –/76. 36.1 t.

156 401	m	**NR**	P	*NO*	NH	52401	57401
156 402	†	**NR**	P	*NO*	NH	52402	57402
156 403	m	**NR**	P	*NO*	NH	52403	57403
156 404	m	**NR**	P	*NO*	NH	52404	57404
156 405	m	**NR**	P	*NO*	NH	52405	57405
156 406	m	**NR**	P	*NO*	NH	52406	57406
156 408	m	**NR**	P	*NO*	NH	52408	57408
156 409	m	**NR**	P	*NO*	NH	52409	57409
156 410	m	**NR**	P	*NO*	NH	52410	57410
156 411	m	**NR**	P	*NO*	NH	52411	57411
156 412	†	**NR**	P	*NO*	NH	52412	57412
156 413	m	**NR**	P	*NO*	NH	52413	57413
156 414	m	**NR**	P	*NO*	NH	52414	57414
156 415	m	**NR**	P	*NO*	NH	52415	57415
156 416	†	**NR**	P	*NO*	NH	52416	57416
156 417	†	**NR**	P	*NO*	NH	52417	57417
156 418	†	**NR**	P	*NO*	NH	52418	57418
156 419	†	**NR**	P	*NO*	NH	52419	57419
156 420	§	**NR**	P	*NO*	NH	52420	57420
156 421	§	**NR**	P	*NO*	HT	52421	57421
156 422	†	**NR**	P	*NO*	NH	52422	57422

156 423	§	**NR**	P	*NO*	NH	52423	57423
156 424	§	**NR**	P	*NO*	NH	52424	57424
156 425	§	**NR**	P	*NO*	NH	52425	57425
156 426	§	**NR**	P	*NO*	NH	52426	57426
156 427	§	**NR**	P	*NO*	NH	52427	57427
156 428	§	**NR**	P	*NO*	NH	52428	57428
156 429	§	**NR**	P	*NO*	NH	52429	57429
156 430	w	**SR**	A	*SR*	CK	52430	57430
156 431	w	**SR**	A	*SR*	CK	52431	57431
156 432	w	**SR**	A	*SR*	CK	52432	57432
156 433	w	**SR**	A	*SR*	CK	52433	57433
156 434	w	**SR**	A	*SR*	CK	52434	57434
156 435	w	**SR**	A	*SR*	CK	52435	57435
156 436	w	**SR**	A	*SR*	CK	52436	57436
156 437	w	**SR**	A	*SR*	CK	52437	57437
156 438	*	**NR**	A	*NO*	HT	52438	57438
156 439	w	**SR**	A	*SR*	CK	52439	57439
156 440	§	**NR**	P	*NO*	HT	52440	57440
156 441	§	**NR**	P	*NO*	NH	52441	57441
156 442	w	**SR**	A	*SR*	CK	52442	57442
156 443	*	**NR**	A	*NO*	HT	52443	57443
156 444	*	**NR**	A	*NO*	HT	52444	57444
156 445	rw	**SR**	A	*SR*	CK	52445	57445
156 446	rw	**SR**	A	*SR*	CK	52446	57446
156 447	n	**NR**	A	*NO*	HT	52447	57447
156 448	*	**NR**	A	*NO*	HT	52448	57448
156 449	n	**NR**	A	*NO*	HT	52449	57449
156 450	rw	**SR**	A	*SR*	CK	52450	57450
156 451	*	**NR**	A	*NO*	HT	52451	57451
156 452	§	**NR**	P	*NO*	NH	52452	57452
156 453	rw	**SR**	A	*SR*	CK	52453	57453
156 454	*	**NR**	A	*NO*	HT	52454	57454
156 455	§	**NR**	P	*NO*	NH	52455	57455
156 456	rw	**SR**	A	*SR*	CK	52456	57456
156 457	rw	**SR**	A	*SR*	CK	52457	57457
156 458	rw	**SR**	A	*SR*	CK	52458	57458
156 459	§	**NR**	P	*NO*	NH	52459	57459
156 460	§	**NR**	P	*NO*	NH	52460	57460
156 461	§	**NR**	P	*NO*	NH	52461	57461
156 462	w	**SR**	A	*SR*	CK	52462	57462
156 463	*	**NR**	A	*NO*	HT	52463	57463
156 464	§	**NR**	P	*NO*	NH	52464	57464
156 465	n	**NR**	A	*NO*	HT	52465	57465
156 466	§	**NR**	P	*NO*	NH	52466	57466
156 467	w	**SR**	A	*SR*	CK	52467	57467
156 468	*	**NR**	A	*NO*	HT	52468	57468
156 469	*	**NR**	A	*NO*	HT	52469	57469
156 470	m	**EM**	A		EP	52470	57470
156 471	*	**NR**	A	*NO*	HT	52471	57471
156 472	*	**NR**	A	*NO*	HT	52472	57472

156 473	m	**EM**	A		EP	52473	57473
156 474	rw	**SR**	A	*SR*	CK	52474	57474
156 475	*	**NR**	A	*NO*	HT	52475	57475
156 476	rw	**SR**	A	*SR*	CK	52476	57476
156 477	rw	**SR**	A	*SR*	CK	52477	57477
156 478	rb	**SR**	BR		ZK	52478	57478
156 479	*	**NR**	A	*NO*	HT	52479	57479
156 480	*	**NR**	A	*NO*	HT	52480	57480
156 481	*	**NR**	A	*NO*	HT	52481	57481
156 482	*	**NR**	A	*NO*	HT	52482	57482
156 483	*	**NR**	A	*NO*	HT	52483	57483
156 484	*	**NR**	A	*NO*	HT	52484	57484
156 485	n	**NR**	A	*NO*	HT	52485	57485
156 486	*	**NR**	A	*NO*	HT	52486	57486
156 487	*	**NR**	A	*NO*	HT	52487	57487
156 488	*	**NR**	A	*NO*	HT	52488	57488
156 489	*	**NR**	A	*NO*	HT	52489	57489
156 490	*	**NR**	A	*NO*	HT	52490	57490
156 491	*	**NR**	A	*NO*	HT	52491	57491
156 492	rw	**SR**	A	*SR*	CK	52492	57492
156 493	rw	**SR**	A	*SR*	CK	52493	57493
156 494	w	**SR**	A	*SR*	CK	52494	57494
156 495	w	**SR**	A	*SR*	CK	52495	57495
156 496	n	**NR**	A	*NO*	HT	52496	57496
156 497	m	**EM**	A		EP	52497	57497
156 498	m	**EM**	A		EP	52498	57498
156 499	rt	**SR**	A	*SR*	CK	52499	57499
156 500	rw	**SR**	A	*SR*	CK	52500	57500
156 501	w	**SR**	A	*SR*	CK	52501	57501
156 502	w	**SR**	A	*SR*	CK	52502	57502
156 503	w	**SR**	A	*SR*	CK	52503	57503
156 504	w	**SR**	A	*SR*	CK	52504	57504
156 505	w	**SR**	A	*SR*	CK	52505	57505
156 506	w	**SR**	A	*SR*	CK	52506	57506
156 507	w	**SR**	A	*SR*	CK	52507	57507
156 508	w	**SR**	A	*SR*	CK	52508	57508
156 509	w	**SR**	A	*SR*	CK	52509	57509
156 510	w	**SR**	A	*SR*	CK	52510	57510
156 511	w	**SR**	A	*SR*	CK	52511	57511
156 512	w	**SR**	A	*SR*	CK	52512	57512
156 513	w	**SR**	A	*SR*	CK	52513	57513
156 514	w	**SR**	A	*SR*	CK	52514	57514

Names:

156 469	The Royal Northumberland Fusiliers (The Fighting Fifth)
156 480	Spirit of The Royal Air Force
156 483	William George 'Billy' Hardy 14/01/1903 – 10/03/1950

Class 156/9. Former Greater Anglia units now in storage.

| 156 907 | (156 407) | † | **EI** | P | | LM | 52407 | 57407 |

CLASS 158/0   BREL

DMSL(B)–DMSL(A) or DMCL–DMSL or DMSL–MSL–DMSL.

Construction: Welded aluminium.
Engines: 158 701–813/158 880–890/158 950–959: One Cummins NTA855R1 of 260 kW (350 hp) at 2100 rpm.
158 815–862: One Perkins 2006-TWH of 260 kW (350 hp) at 2100 rpm.
158 863–872: One Cummins NTA855R3 of 300 kW (400 hp) at 1900 rpm.
Bogies: One BREL P4 (powered) and one BREL T4 (non-powered) per car.
Couplers: BSI.   **Dimensions:** 22.57 x 2.70 m.
Gangways: Throughout.   **Wheel Arrangement:** 2-B + B-2.
Doors: Twin-leaf swing plug.   **Maximum Speed:** 90 mph.
Seating Layout: 2+2 facing/unidirectional.
Multiple Working: Within class and with Classes 142, 143, 144, 150, 153, 155, 156, 159, 170 and 172.

ScotRail 158s 158 701–736/738–741 are "fitted" for RETB. When a unit arrives at Inverness the cab display unit is clipped on and plugged in.
Transport for Wales units have ETCS plugged in at Shrewsbury for working the Cambrian Lines.

*   Refurbished ScotRail units fitted with Grammer seating, additional luggage racks and cycle stowage areas.
     ScotRail units 158 726–736/738–741 are fitted with Richmond seating.
†   Refurbished East Midlands Railway units with Grammer seating.
§   Northern 3-car units (original seating).
n   Refurbished Northern units with new Fainsa seating.
p   Refurbished ScotRail units with Richmond seating.
s   Refurbished Transport for Wales units with Grammer seating.
z   Refurbished Great Western Railway units. Units 158 745–749/751/762/ 767 (some formed into 3-car sets) have Richmond seating.

DMSL(B). Lot No. 31051 BREL Derby 1989–92. † 68(+3) 1TD 2W, § –/64(+3) 1TD 2W, n –/66 1TD 2W, s –/64(+4) 1TD 2W, z –/62 1TD 2W. 38.5 t.
MSL. Lot No. 31050 BREL Derby 1991. –/68 1T. 38.5 t.
DMSL(A). Lot No. 31052 BREL Derby 1989–92. –/70 1T († –/74, n –/72 1T, * & p –/64(+2) 1T, z –/68) plus cycle stowage area. 38.5 t.

The above details refer to the "as built" condition. The following DMSL(B) have now been converted to DMCL as follows:
52701–736/738–741 (ScotRail). 15/53 1TD 1W (* refurbished sets –/60(+6) 1TD 1W plus cycle stowage area).

158 701	*	**SR**	P	*SR*	IS	52701 57701
158 702	*	**SR**	P	*SR*	IS	52702 57702
158 703	*	**SR**	P	*SR*	IS	52703 57703
158 704	*	**SR**	P	*SR*	IS	52704 57704
158 705	*	**SR**	P	*SR*	IS	52705 57705
158 706	*	**SR**	P	*SR*	IS	52706 57706
158 707	*	**SR**	P	*SR*	IS	52707 57707
158 708	*	**SR**	P	*SR*	IS	52708 57708
158 709	*	**SR**	P	*SR*	IS	52709 57709

158 710	*	**SR**	P	*SR*	IS	52710	57710
158 711	*	**SR**	P	*SR*	IS	52711	57711
158 712	*	**SR**	P	*SR*	IS	52712	57712
158 713	*	**SR**	P	*SR*	IS	52713	57713
158 714	*	**SR**	P	*SR*	IS	52714	57714
158 715	*	**SR**	P	*SR*	IS	52715	57715
158 716	*	**SR**	P	*SR*	IS	52716	57716
158 717	*	**SR**	P	*SR*	IS	52717	57717
158 718	*	**SR**	P	*SR*	IS	52718	57718
158 719	*	**SR**	P	*SR*	IS	52719	57719
158 720	*	**SR**	P	*SR*	IS	52720	57720
158 721	*	**SR**	P	*SR*	IS	52721	57721
158 722	*	**SR**	P	*SR*	IS	52722	57722
158 723	*	**SR**	P	*SR*	IS	52723	57723
158 724	*	**SR**	P	*SR*	IS	52724	57724
158 725	*	**SR**	P	*SR*	IS	52725	57725
158 726	p	**SR**	P	*SR*	CK	52726	57726
158 727	p	**SR**	P	*SR*	CK	52727	57727
158 728	p	**SR**	P	*SR*	CK	52728	57728
158 729	p	**SR**	P	*SR*	CK	52729	57729
158 730	p	**SR**	P	*SR*	CK	52730	57730
158 731	p	**SR**	P	*SR*	CK	52731	57731
158 732	p	**SR**	P	*SR*	CK	52732	57732
158 733	p	**SR**	P	*SR*	CK	52733	57733
158 734	p	**SR**	P	*SR*	CK	52734	57734
158 735	p	**SR**	P	*SR*	CK	52735	57735
158 736	p	**SR**	P	*SR*	CK	52736	57736
158 738	p	**SR**	P	*SR*	CK	52738	57738
158 739	p	**SR**	P	*SR*	CK	52739	57739
158 740	p	**SR**	P	*SR*	CK	52740	57740
158 741	p	**SR**	P	*SR*	CK	52741	57741
158 745	z	**GW**	P	*GW*	PM	52745	57745
158 747	z	**GW**	P	*GW*	PM	52747	57747
158 748	z	**GW**	P	*GW*	PM	52748	57748
158 749	z	**GW**	P	*GW*	PM	52749	57749
158 750	z	**GW**	P	*GW*	PM	52750	57750
158 752	§	**NR**	P	*NO*	NL	52752	58716	57752
158 753	§	**NR**	P	*NO*	NL	52753	58710	57753
158 754	§	**NR**	P	*NO*	NL	52754	58708	57754
158 755	§	**NR**	P	*NO*	NL	52755	58702	57755
158 756	§	**NR**	P	*NO*	NL	52756	58712	57756
158 757	§	**NR**	P	*NO*	NL	52757	58706	57757
158 758	§	**NR**	P	*NO*	NL	52758	58714	57758
158 759	§	**NR**	P	*NO*	NL	52759	58713	57759
158 760	z	**GW**	P	*GW*	PM	52760	57760
158 762	z	**GW**	P	*GW*	PM	52762	57762
158 765	z	**GW**	P	*GW*	PM	52765	57765
158 766	z	**GW**	P	*GW*	PM	52766	57766
158 767	z	**GW**	P	*GW*	PM	52767	57767
158 768	z	**GW**	P	*GW*	PM	52768	57768
158 769	z	**GW**	P	*GW*	PM	52769	57769

158 770	†	**ST**	P	*EM*	NM	52770	57770
158 771	z	**GW**	P	*GW*	PM	52771	57771
158 773	†	**EI**	P	*EM*	NM	52773	57773
158 774	†	**EI**	P	*EM*	NM	52774	57774
158 777	†	**ST**	P	*EM*	NM	52777	57777
158 780	†	**ST**	A	*EM*	NM	52780	57780
158 782	n	**NR**	A	*NO*	NL	52782	57782
158 783	†	**ST**	A	*EM*	NM	52783	57783
158 784	n	**NR**	A	*NO*	NL	52784	57784
158 785	†	**ST**	A	*EM*	NM	52785	57785
158 786	n	**NR**	A	*NO*	NL	52786	57786
158 787	n	**NR**	A	*NO*	NL	52787	57787
158 788	†	**ST**	A	*EM*	NM	52788	57788
158 789	n	**NR**	A	*NO*	NL	52789	57789
158 790	n	**NR**	A	*NO*	NL	52790	57790
158 791	n	**NR**	A	*NO*	NL	52791	57791
158 792	n	**NR**	A	*NO*	HT	52792	57792
158 793	n	**NR**	A	*NO*	NL	52793	57793
158 794	n	**NR**	A	*NO*	NL	52794	57794
158 795	n	**NR**	A	*NO*	NL	52795	57795
158 796	n	**NR**	A	*NO*	NL	52796	57796
158 797	n	**NR**	A	*NO*	NL	52797	57797
158 798	z	**GW**	P	*GW*	EX	52798	58715	57798
158 799	†	**ST**	P	*EM*	NM	52799	57799
158 806	†	**ST**	P	*EM*	NM	52806	57806
158 810	†	**ST**	P	*EM*	NM	52810	57810
158 812	†	**ST**	P	*EM*	NM	52812	57812
158 813	†	**ST**	P	*EM*	NM	52813	57813
158 815	n	**NR**	A	*NO*	HT	52815	57815
158 816	n	**NR**	A	*NO*	HT	52816	57816
158 817	n	**NR**	A	*NO*	HT	52817	57817
158 818	es	**TW**	A	*TW*	MN	52818	57818
158 819	es	**TW**	A	*TW*	MN	52819	57819
158 820	es	**TW**	A	*TW*	MN	52820	57820
158 821	es	**TW**	A	*TW*	MN	52821	57821
158 822	es	**TW**	A	*TW*	MN	52822	57822
158 823	es	**TW**	A	*TW*	MN	52823	57823
158 824	es	**TW**	A	*TW*	MN	52824	57824
158 825	es	**TW**	A	*TW*	MN	52825	57825
158 826	es	**TW**	A	*TW*	MN	52826	57826
158 827	es	**TW**	A	*TW*	MN	52827	57827
158 828	es	**TW**	A	*TW*	MN	52828	57828
158 829	es	**TW**	A	*TW*	MN	52829	57829
158 830	es	**TW**	A	*TW*	MN	52830	57830
158 831	es	**TW**	A	*TW*	MN	52831	57831
158 832	es	**TW**	A	*TW*	MN	52832	57832
158 833	es	**TW**	A	*TW*	MN	52833	57833
158 834	es	**TW**	A	*TW*	MN	52834	57834
158 835	es	**TW**	A	*TW*	MN	52835	57835
158 836	es	**TW**	A	*TW*	MN	52836	57836
158 837	es	**TW**	A	*TW*	MN	52837	57837

158 838	es	**TW**	A	*TW*	MN	52838	57838
158 839	es	**TW**	A	*TW*	MN	52839	57839
158 840	es	**TW**	A	*TW*	MN	52840	57840
158 841	es	**TW**	A	*TW*	MN	52841	57841
158 842	n	**NR**	A	*NO*	HT	52842	57842
158 843	n	**NR**	A	*NO*	HT	52843	57843
158 844	n	**NR**	A	*NO*	HT	52844	57844
158 845	n	**NR**	A	*NO*	HT	52845	57845
158 846	†	**ST**	A	*EM*	NM	52846	57846
158 847	†	**ST**	A	*EM*	NM	52847	57847
158 848	n	**NR**	A	*NO*	HT	52848	57848
158 849	n	**NR**	A	*NO*	HT	52849	57849
158 850	n	**NR**	A	*NO*	HT	52850	57850
158 851	n	**NR**	A	*NO*	HT	52851	57851
158 852	†	**ST**	A	*EM*	NM	52852	57852
158 853	n	**NR**	A	*NO*	HT	52853	57853
158 854	†	**ST**	A	*EM*	NM	52854	57854
158 855	n	**NR**	A	*NO*	HT	52855	57855
158 856	†	**ST**	A	*EM*	NM	52856	57856
158 857	†	**ST**	A	*EM*	NM	52857	57857
158 858	†	**ST**	A	*EM*	NM	52858	57858
158 859	n	**NR**	A	*NO*	HT	52859	57859
158 860	n	**NR**	A	*NO*	HT	52860	57860
158 861	n	**NR**	A	*NO*	HT	52861	57861
158 862	†	**ST**	A	*EM*	NM	52862	57862
158 863	†	**ST**	A	*EM*	NM	52863	57863
158 864	†	**ST**	A	*EM*	NM	52864	57864
158 865	†	**ST**	A	*EM*	NM	52865	57865
158 866	†	**ST**	A	*EM*	NM	52866	57866
158 867	n	**NR**	A	*NO*	NL	52867	57867
158 868	n	**NR**	A	*NO*	NL	52868	57868
158 869	n	**NR**	A	*NO*	NL	52869	57869
158 870	n	**NR**	A	*NO*	NL	52870	57870
158 871	n	**NR**	A	*NO*	NL	52871	57871
158 872	n	**NR**	A	*NO*	NL	52872	57872

Names:

158 847	Lincoln Castle Explorer
158 854	The Station Volunteer
158 864	ELR 50 VISIT LINCOLNSHIRE in 2020

Class 158/8. Refurbished South Western Railway and East Midlands Railway units. Converted from former TransPennine Express units at Wabtec, Doncaster in 2007. 2+1 seating in First Class.

Details as Class 158/0 except:

DMCL. Lot No. 31051 BREL Derby 1989–92. 13/40(+2) 1TD 1W. 38.5 t.
DMSL. Lot No. 31052 BREL Derby 1989–92. –/70 1T. 38.5 t.

158 880	(158 737)	**ST**	P	*SW*	SA	52737	57737
158 881	(158 742)	**ST**	P	*SW*	SA	52742	57742
158 882	(158 743)	**ST**	P	*SW*	SA	52743	57743

158 883	(158 744)	**ST**	P	*SW*	SA	52744	57744
158 884	(158 772)	**ST**	P	*SW*	SA	52772	57772
158 885	(158 775)	**ST**	P	*SW*	SA	52775	57775
158 886	(158 779)	**ST**	P	*SW*	SA	52779	57779
158 887	(158 781)	**SW**	P	*SW*	SA	52781	57781
158 888	(158 802)	**SW**	P	*SW*	SA	52802	57802
158 889	(158 808)	**ST**	P	*EM*	NM	52808	57808
158 890	(158 814)	**SW**	P	*SW*	SA	52814	57814

CLASS 158/9   BREL

DMSL–DMS. Units leased by West Yorkshire PTE but managed by Eversholt Rail. Refurbished with new Fainsa seating. Details as Class 158/0 except for seating and toilets.

DMSL. Lot No. 31051 BREL Derby 1990–92. –/66 1TD 2W. 38.5 t.
DMS. Lot No. 31052 BREL Derby 1990–92. –/72 and parcels area. 38.5 t.

158 901	**NR**	E	*NO*	NL	52901	57901
158 902	**NR**	E	*NO*	NL	52902	57902
158 903	**NR**	E	*NO*	NL	52903	57903
158 904	**NR**	E	*NO*	NL	52904	57904
158 905	**NR**	E	*NO*	NL	52905	57905
158 906	**NR**	E	*NO*	NL	52906	57906
158 907	**NR**	E	*NO*	NL	52907	57907
158 908	**NR**	E	*NO*	NL	52908	57908
158 909	**NR**	E	*NO*	NL	52909	57909
158 910	**NR**	E	*NO*	NL	52910	57910

CLASS 158/0   BREL

DMSL(A)–DMSL(B)–DMSL(A). Units reformed as 3-car hybrid sets for Great Western Railway. For vehicle details see above. Formations can be flexible depending on when unit exams become due.

158 950	**GW**	P	*GW*	EX	57751	52761	57761
158 951	**GW**	P	*GW*	EX	52751	52764	57764
158 958	**GW**	P	*GW*	EX	57746	52776	57776
158 959	**GW**	P	*GW*	EX	52746	52778	57778

CLASS 159/0   BREL

DMCL–MSL–DMSL. Built as Class 158. Converted before entering passenger service to Class 159 by Rosyth Dockyard.

Construction: Welded aluminium.
Engines: One Cummins NTA855R3 of 300 kW (400 hp) at 1900 rpm.
Bogies: One BREL P4 (powered) and one BREL T4 (non-powered) per car.
Couplers: BSI.   **Dimensions:** 22.57 x 2.70 m.
Gangways: Throughout.   **Wheel Arrangement:** 2-B + B-2 + B-2.
Doors: Twin-leaf swing plug.   **Maximum Speed:** 90 mph.

Seating Layout: 1: 2+1 facing, 2: 2+2 facing/unidirectional.
Multiple Working: Within class and with Classes 142, 143, 144, 150, 153, 155, 156, 158 and 170.

DMCL. Lot No. 31051 BREL Derby 1992–93. 23/24(+2) 1TD 2W. 38.5 t.
MSL. Lot No. 31050 BREL Derby 1992–93. –/70(+6) 1T. 38.5 t.
DMSL. Lot No. 31052 BREL Derby 1992–93. –/72 1T. 38.5 t.

159 001	**SW**	P	*SW*	SA	52873	58718	57873
159 002	**SW**	P	*SW*	SA	52874	58719	57874
159 003	**SW**	P	*SW*	SA	52875	58720	57875
159 004	**SW**	P	*SW*	SA	52876	58721	57876
159 005	**SW**	P	*SW*	SA	52877	58722	57877
159 006	**SW**	P	*SW*	SA	52878	58723	57878
159 007	**SW**	P	*SW*	SA	52879	58724	57879
159 008	**SW**	P	*SW*	SA	52880	58725	57880
159 009	**SW**	P	*SW*	SA	52881	58726	57881
159 010	**SW**	P	*SW*	SA	52882	58727	57882
159 011	**SW**	P	*SW*	SA	52883	58728	57883
159 012	**SW**	P	*SW*	SA	52884	58729	57884
159 013	**SW**	P	*SW*	SA	52885	58730	57885
159 014	**SW**	P	*SW*	SA	52886	58731	57886
159 015	**SW**	P	*SW*	SA	52887	58732	57887
159 016	**SW**	P	*SW*	SA	52888	58733	57888
159 017	**SW**	P	*SW*	SA	52889	58734	57889
159 018	**SW**	P	*SW*	SA	52890	58735	57890
159 019	**SW**	P	*SW*	SA	52891	58736	57891
159 020	**SW**	P	*SW*	SA	52892	58737	57892
159 021	**SW**	P	*SW*	SA	52893	58738	57893
159 022	**SW**	P	*SW*	SA	52894	58739	57894

CLASS 159/1   BREL

DMCL–MSL–DMSL. Units converted from Class 158s at Wabtec, Doncaster in 2006–07 for South West Trains.

Details as Class 158/0 except:
Seating Layout: 1: 2+1 facing, 2: 2+2 facing/unidirectional.

DMCL. Lot No. 31051 BREL Derby 1989–92. 24/24(+2) 1TD 2W. 38.5 t.
MSL. Lot No. 31050 BREL Derby 1989–92. –/70 1T. 38.5 t.
DMSL. Lot No. 31052 BREL Derby 1989–92. –/72 1T. 38.5 t.

159 101	(158 800)	**ST**	P	*SW*	SA	52800	58717	57800
159 103	(158 804)	**ST**	P	*SW*	SA	52804	58704	57804
159 104	(158 805)	**ST**	P	*SW*	SA	52805	58705	57805
159 105	(158 807)	**ST**	P	*SW*	SA	52807	58707	57807
159 106	(158 809)	**ST**	P	*SW*	SA	52809	58709	57809
159 107	(158 811)	**ST**	P	*SW*	SA	52811	58711	57811
159 108	(158 801)	**ST**	P	*SW*	SA	52801	58701	57801
Spare		**ST**	P		LM	52803		

CLASS 165/0   NETWORK TURBO   BREL

DMSL–DMS and DMSL–MS–DMS. Chiltern Railways units. Refurbished 2003–05 with First Class seats removed and air conditioning fitted.

Construction: Welded aluminium.
Engines: One Perkins 2006-TWH of 260 kW (350 hp) at 2100 rpm.
Bogies: BREL P3-17 (powered), BREL T3-17 (non-powered).
Couplers: BSI.
Dimensions: 23.50/23.25 x 2.81 m.
Gangways: Within unit only.   **Wheel Arrangement:** 2-B (+ B-2) + B-2.
Doors: Twin-leaf swing plug.   **Maximum Speed:** 75 mph.
Seating Layout: 2+2/3+2 facing/unidirectional.
Multiple Working: Within class and with Classes 166, 168, 170 and 172.

Fitted with tripcocks for working over London Underground tracks between Harrow-on-the-Hill and Amersham.

58801–822/58873–878. DMSL. Lot No. 31087 BREL York 1990. –/77(+7) 1TD 2W. 42.1 t.
58823–833. DMSL. Lot No. 31089 BREL York 1991–92. –/77(+7) 1TD 2W. 40.1 t.
MS. Lot No. 31090 BREL York 1991–92. –/106. 37.0 t.
DMS. Lot No. 31088 BREL York 1991–92. –/94. 41.5 t.

165 001	CR	A	CR	AL	58801	58834
165 002	CR	A	CR	AL	58802	58835
165 003	CR	A	CR	AL	58803	58836
165 004	CR	A	CR	AL	58804	58837
165 005	CR	A	CR	AL	58805	58838
165 006	CR	A	CR	AL	58806	58839
165 007	CR	A	CR	AL	58807	58840
165 008	CR	A	CR	AL	58808	58841
165 009	CR	A	CR	AL	58809	58842
165 010	CR	A	CR	AL	58810	58843
165 011	CR	A	CR	AL	58811	58844
165 012	CR	A	CR	AL	58812	58845
165 013	CR	A	CR	AL	58813	58846
165 014	CR	A	CR	AL	58814	58847
165 015	CR	A	CR	AL	58815	58848
165 016	CR	A	CR	AL	58816	58849
165 017	CR	A	CR	AL	58817	58850
165 018	CR	A	CR	AL	58818	58851
165 019	CR	A	CR	AL	58819	58852
165 020	CR	A	CR	AL	58820	58853
165 021	CR	A	CR	AL	58821	58854
165 022	CR	A	CR	AL	58822	58855
165 023	CR	A	CR	AL	58873	58867
165 024	CR	A	CH	AL	58074	58868
165 025	CR	A	CR	AL	58875	58869
165 026	CR	A	CR	AL	58876	58870
165 027	CR	A	CR	AL	58877	58871
165 028	CR	A	CR	AL	58878	58872

165 029	**CR**	A	*CR*	AL	58823	55404	58856
165 030	**CR**	A	*CR*	AL	58824	55405	58857
165 031	**CR**	A	*CR*	AL	58825	55406	58858
165 032	**CR**	A	*CR*	AL	58826	55407	58859
165 033	**CR**	A	*CR*	AL	58827	55408	58860
165 034	**CR**	A	*CR*	AL	58828	55409	58861
165 035	**CR**	A	*CR*	AL	58829	55410	58862
165 036	**CR**	A	*CR*	AL	58830	55411	58863
165 037	**CR**	A	*CR*	AL	58831	55412	58864
165 038	**CR**	A	*CR*	AL	58832	55413	58865
165 039	**CR**	A	*CR*	AL	58833	55414	58866

CLASS 165/1   NETWORK TURBO   BREL

Great Western Railway units. DMSL–MS–DMS or DMSL–DMS. In 2015 GWR removed First Class from all its Class 165s, it was later reinstated on the 3-car units. Air cooling equipment fitted.

Construction: Welded aluminium.
Engines: One Perkins 2006-TWH of 260 kW (350 hp) at 2100 rpm.
Bogies: BREL P3-17 (powered), BREL T3-17 (non-powered).
Couplers: BSI.
Dimensions: 23.50/23.25 x 2.81 m.
Gangways: Within unit only.   **Wheel Arrangement:** 2-B (+ B-2) + B-2.
Doors: Twin-leaf swing plug.   **Maximum Speed:** 90 mph.
Seating Layout: 3+2/2+2 facing/unidirectional.
Multiple Working: Within class and with Classes 166, 168, 170 and 172.

58953–969. DMSL. Lot No. 31098 BREL York 1992. 16/44 1TD 2W. 40.8 t.
58879–898. DMSL. Lot No. 31096 BREL York 1992. –/75 1TD 2W. 40.8 t.
MS. Lot No. 31099 BREL 1992. –/102. 38.1 t.
58916–932. DMS. Lot No. 31097 BREL 1992. –/98. 37.0 t.
58933–952. DMS. Lot No. 31097 BREL 1992. –/84. 37.0 t.

165 101	**GW**	A	*GW*	PM	58953	55415	58916
165 102	**GW**	A	*GW*	PM	58954	55416	58917
165 103	**GW**	A	*GW*	RG	58955	55417	58918
165 104	**GW**	A	*GW*	RG	58956	55418	58919
165 105	**GW**	A	*GW*	RG	58957	55419	58920
165 106	**GW**	A	*GW*	RG	58958	55420	58921
165 107	**GW**	A	*GW*	RG	58959	55421	58922
165 108	**GW**	A	*GW*	PM	58960	55422	58923
165 109	**GW**	A	*GW*	RG	58961	55423	58924
165 110	**GW**	A	*GW*	RG	58962	55424	58925
165 111	**GW**	A	*GW*	RG	58963	55425	58926
165 112	**GW**	A	*GW*	PM	58964	55426	58927
165 113	**GW**	A	*GW*	RG	58965	55427	58928
165 114	**GW**	A	*GW*	RG	58966	55428	58929
165 116	**GW**	A	*GW*	RG	58968	55430	58931
165 117	**GW**	A	*GW*	RG	58969	55431	58932
165 118	**GW**	A	*GW*	RG	58879		58933
165 119	**GW**	A	*GW*	RG	58880		58934

165 120	**GW**	A	*GW*	RG	58881	58935
165 121	**GW**	A	*GW*	RG	58882	58936
165 122	**GW**	A	*GW*	RG	58883	58937
165 123	**GW**	A	*GW*	RG	58884	58938
165 124	**GW**	A	*GW*	RG	58885	58939
165 125	**GW**	A	*GW*	RG	58886	58940
165 126	**GW**	A	*GW*	RG	58887	58941
165 127	**GW**	A	*GW*	RG	58888	58942
165 128	**GW**	A	*GW*	RG	58889	58943
165 129	**GW**	A	*GW*	RG	58890	58944
165 130	**GW**	A	*GW*	PM	58891	58945
165 131	**GW**	A	*GW*	PM	58892	58946
165 132	**GW**	A	*GW*	PM	58893	58947
165 133	**GW**	A	*GW*	PM	58894	58948
165 134	**GW**	A	*GW*	PM	58895	58949
165 135	**GW**	A	*GW*	PM	58896	58950
165 136	**GW**	A	*GW*	PM	58897	58951
165 137	**GW**	A	*GW*	PM	58898	58952

Names:

165 119	Norman Topsom MBE
165 120	Roger Watkins THE GWR MASTER TRAIN PLANNER

CLASS 166   NETWORK EXPRESS TURBO   ABB

DMCL–MS–DMSL. Great Western Railway units, built for Paddington–Oxford/Newbury services. Air conditioned and with additional luggage space compared to the Class 165s. The DMSL vehicles have had their 16 First Class seats declassified.

Construction: Welded aluminium.
Engines: One Perkins 2006-TWH of 260 kW (350 hp) at 2100 rpm.
Bogies: BREL P3-17 (powered), BREL T3-17 (non-powered).
Couplers: BSI.
Dimensions: 23.50 x 2.81 m.
Gangways: Within unit only.   **Wheel Arrangement:** 2-B + B-2 + B-2.
Doors: Twin-leaf swing plug.   **Maximum Speed:** 90 mph.
Seating Layout: 1: 2+2 facing, 2: 2+2/3+2 facing/unidirectional.
Multiple Working: Within class and with Classes 165, 168, 170 and 172.

DMCL. Lot No. 31116 ABB York 1992–93. 16/53 1TD 2W. 41.2 t.
MS. Lot No. 31117 ABB York 1992–93. –/91. 39.9 t.
DMSL. Lot No. 31116 ABB York 1992–93. –/84 1T. 39.6 t.

166 201	**GW**	A	*GW*	PM	58101	58601	58122
166 202	**GW**	A	*GW*	PM	58102	58602	58123
166 203	**GW**	A	*GW*	PM	58103	58603	58124
166 204	**GW**	A	*GW*	PM	58104	58604	58125
166 205	**GW**	A	*GW*	PM	58105	58605	58126
166 206	**GW**	A	*GW*	PM	58106	58606	5812/
166 207	**FB**	A	*GW*	PM	58107	58607	58128
166 208	**GW**	A	*GW*	PM	58108	58608	58129
166 209	**FB**	A	*GW*	PM	58109	58609	58130

▲ The Swanage Railway's Class 117 (51388/59486/51356) and Class 121 55028 are registered for use on the national network from Worgret Jn to Wareham. Here they arrive at Wareham with the 12.14 from Swanage on 05/09/23. **Tony Christie**

▼ BR carmine & cream-liveried 121 022 (55022) arrives at Glenfinnan with a Locomotive Services special to Arisaig on 28/09/23. **Mike Heath**

▲ West Midlands Railway-liveried Parry People Mover 139 001 arrives at Stourbridge Junction with the 10.20 shuttle from Stourbridge Town on 13/06/21.
Jamie Squibbs

▼ Greater Manchester PTE-liveried 142 003, owned by Locomotive Services, is seen at Llandudno after arrival with the "Saint Tudno Wanderer" railtour from Wilmslow on 27/09/23.
Paul Beardsley

▲ London Northwestern Railway-liveried 150137 passes Husborne Crawley, near Ridgmont, with the 09.45 Bletchley–Bedford crew training run prior to the resumption of services on the Marston Vale Line on 22/09/23. **Mark Beal**

▼ Converted to a Network Rail Inspection Train, light blue liveried 153376 passes Lower Hartburn with 2Q21 09.47 Doncaster–Doncaster on 17/08/23. **Alex Ayre**

▲ Northern-liveried 155344 is seen near Anlaby Road Junction (Hull) with the 09.45 York–Bridlington on 28/09/21. **Robin Ralston**

▼ ScotRail-liveried 156457 and 156431 leave Glasgow Central with the 16.47 to East Kilbride on 09/06/23. **Robert Pritchard**

▲ East Midlands Railway (interim)-liveried 158773 (with Pride stripes) leads Stagecoach-liveried 158799 on the 14.51 Liverpool Lime Street–Norwich away from Sheffield on 24/06/23. **Robert Pritchard**

▼ South Western Railway-liveried 159017 and 159014 pass Queenstown Road Battersea with the 17.53 London Waterloo–Yeovil Junction on 07/06/23. **Robert Pritchard**

▲ Chiltern Railways-liveried 165 019 passes Neasden with the 17.17 London Marylebone–Oxford on 24/05/22. **Robert Pritchard**

▼ Great Western Railway-liveried 166 214 runs along the sea wall at Dawlish with the 07.39 Paignton–Exmouth on 07/06/23. **Robert Pritchard**

▲ Chiltern Railways Mainline-liveried 168 323 and 168 108 leave Haddenham & Thame Parkway with the 08.00 London Marylebone–Birmingham Moor Street on 09/04/22. **Robert Pritchard**

▼ CrossCountry-liveried 170 103 is seen at Nottingham with the 15.07 to Cardiff Central on 12/06/23. **Robert Pritchard**

▲ Southern-liveried 171802 passes Redhill with an empty stock working on 18/07/23. **Alex Dasi-Sutton**

▼ West Midlands Railway-liveried 172214 and 172218 call at The Hawthorns with the 16.03 Dorridge–Worcester Foregate Street on 14/10/22. **Robert Pritchard**

▲ Grand Central-liveried 180102 passes South Otterington on the East Coast Main Line with the 08.53 Sunderland–London King's Cross on 09/08/23. **Alex Ayre**

▼ TransPennine Express-liveried 185116 and 185123 head away from Sheffield with the 10.26 Cleethorpes–Manchester Piccadilly on 22/10/22. **Robert Pritchard**

▲ Northern-liveried 195 105 leaves Sheffield with the 17.14 to Manchester Piccadilly on 16/08/23. **Robert Pritchard**

▼ West Midlands Railway-liveried 196 110 leaves Shrewsbury with the 12.40 to Birmingham New Street on 10/12/22. **Robert Pritchard**

▲ Transport for Wales-liveried 197015 passes East Didsbury with the 12.53 Llandudno Junction–Manchester Airport on 29/05/23. **Robert Pritchard**

▼ Preserved "Hastings" DEMU 1001 is seen at London Bridge with a UK Railtours excursion that visited the 13 London termini on 15/04/23. **Ian Beardsley**

▲ CrossCountry-liveried 220031 and 221123 arrive at Chesterfield with the 12.03 Edinburgh–Plymouth on 16/08/23. **Robert Pritchard**

▼ Avanti West Coast Voyager-liveried 221108 and 221110 approach Gretna Green with the diverted 10.22 Glasgow Central–Carlisle on 08/03/23. **Robin Ralston**

▲ East Midlands Railway interim-liveried 222 103 approaches Dronfield with the 15.02 London St Pancras–Sheffield on 17/08/23. **Robert Pritchard**

▼ Transport for Wales-liveried 230 010 arrives at Gwersyllt with the 14.34 Bidston–Wrexham Central on 13/06/23. **Cliff Beeton**

▲ Transport for Wales-liveried 231008 is seen at Cardiff Central with the 12.28 Ystrad Mynach–Penarth on 19/06/23. **Robert Pritchard**

▼ Swietelsky Babcock Rail Plasser & Theurer Dynamic Tamper DR75012 approaches Wolverton with 6Q60 09.31 Bletchley–Bletchley via Croft on 20/02/23. **Mark Beal**

▲ VolkerRail Matisa B 41 UE Tampers DR 75401 and DR 75402 pass Saxilby with 6J38 10.08 Doncaster–Peterborough on 04/11/22. **Robert Pritchard**

▼ Network Rail Mobile Maintenance Train DR 97804/DR 97604/DR 97504 is seen stabled at Leicester on 14/01/23. **Ian Beardsley**

▲ Network Rail yellow-liveried Track Assessment Unit 950001 runs along the sea wall at Dawlish with 2Q08 03.39 Penzance–Exeter Riverside on 23/08/23. **Robin Ralston**

▼ Network Rail Independent Snowploughs ADB965235 and ADB965223 pass Cogload Junction with 7Z21 11.22 Taunton Fairwater Yard–Weston-super-Mare–Taunton Fairwater Yard test run, powered by 37419 and 37601. **Tony Christie**

166 210	**GW**	A	*GW*	PM	58110	58610	58131
166 211	**FB**	A	*GW*	PM	58111	58611	58132
166 212	**GW**	A	*GW*	PM	58112	58612	58133
166 213	**GW**	A	*GW*	PM	58113	58613	58134
166 214	**GW**	A	*GW*	PM	58114	58614	58135
166 215	**GW**	A	*GW*	PM	58115	58615	58136
166 216	**GW**	A	*GW*	PM	58116	58616	58137
166 217	**GW**	A	*GW*	PM	58117	58617	58138
166 218	**GW**	A	*GW*	PM	58118	58618	58139
166 219	**GW**	A	*GW*	PM	58119	58619	58140
166 220	**GW**	A	*GW*	PM	58120	58620	58141
166 221	**GW**	A	*GW*	PM	58121	58621	58142

Names:

166 204   Norman Topsom MBE
166 220   Roger Watkins THE GWR MASTER TRAIN PLANNER

CLASS 168   CLUBMAN   ADTRANZ/BOMBARDIER

Air conditioned.

Construction: Welded aluminium bodies with bolt-on steel ends.
Engines: One MTU 6R183TD13H of 315 kW (422 hp) at 1900 rpm (*MTU 6H 1800 + MTU EnergyPack battery system for hybrid operation).
Transmission: Hydraulic. Voith T211rzze to ZF final drive.
Bogies: One Adtranz P3–23 and one BREL T3–23 per car.
Couplers: BSI at outer ends, bar within unit.
Dimensions: Class 168/0: 24.10/23.61 x 2.69 m. Others: 23.62/23.61 x 2.69 m.
Gangways: Within unit only.   **Wheel Arrangement:** 2-B (+ B-2 + B-2) + B-2.
Doors: Twin-leaf swing plug.   **Maximum Speed:** 100 mph.
Seating Layout: 2+2 facing/unidirectional.
Multiple Working: Within class and with Classes 165 and 166.

Fitted with tripcocks for working over London Underground tracks between Harrow-on-the-Hill and Amersham.

Non-standard livery: 168329 HybridFLEX (dark blue, green & grey).

Class 168/0. Original Design. DMSL(A)–MS–MSL–DMSL(B) or DMSL(A)–MSL–MS–DMSL(B).

58451–455 were numbered 58656–660 for a time when used in 168 106–110.

58151–155. DMSL(A). Adtranz Derby 1997–98. –/57 1TD 1W. 44.0 t.
58651–655. MSL. Adtranz Derby 1998. –/73 1T. 41.0 t.
58451–455. MS. Adtranz Derby 1998. –/77. 41.0 t.
58251–255. DMSL(B). Adtranz Derby 1998. –/68 1T. 43.6 t.

168 001	**CL**	P	*CR*	AL	58151	58651	58451	58251
168 002	**CL**	P	*CR*	AL	58152	58652	58452	58252
168 003	**CL**	P	*CR*	AL	58153	58453	58653	58253
168 004	**CL**	P	*CR*	AL	58154	58654	58454	58254
168 005	**CL**	P	*CR*	AL	58155	58655	58455	58255

Name: 168001   Adrian Shooter CBE

Class 168/1. These units are effectively Class 170s. DMSL(A)–MSL–MS–DMSL(B) or DMSL(A)–MS–DMSL(B).

58461–463 were renumbered from 58661–663.

58156–163. DMSL(A). Adtranz Derby 2000. –/57 1TD 2W. 45.2 t.
58456–460. MS. Bombardier Derby 2002. –/76. 41.8 t.
58756–757. MSL. Bombardier Derby 2002. –/73 1T. 42.9 t.
58461–463. MS. Adtranz Derby 2000. –/76. 42.4 t.
58256–263. DMSL(B). Adtranz Derby 2000. –/69 1T. 45.2 t.

168 106	**CL**	P	*CR*	AL	58156	58756	58456	58256
168 107	**CL**	P	*CR*	AL	58157	58757	58457	58257
168 108	**CL**	P	*CR*	AL	58158		58458	58258
168 109	**CL**	P	*CR*	AL	58159		58459	58259
168 110	**CL**	P	*CR*	AL	58160		58460	58260
168 111	**CL**	E	*CR*	AL	58161		58461	58261
168 112	**CL**	E	*CR*	AL	58162		58462	58262
168 113	**CL**	E	*CR*	AL	58163		58463	58263

Class 168/2. These units are effectively Class 170s. DMSL(A)–(MS)–MS–DMSL(B).

58164–169. DMSL(A). Bombardier Derby 2003–04. –/57 1TD 2W. 45.4 t.
58365–367. MS. Bombardier Derby 2006. –/76. 43.3 t.
58464/468/469. MS. Bombardier Derby 2003–04. –/76. 44.0 t.
58465–467. MS. Bombardier Derby 2006. –/76. 43.3 t.
58264–269. DMSL(B). Bombardier Derby 2003–04. –/69 1T. 45.5 t.

168 214	**CL**	P	*CR*	AL	58164		58464	58264
168 215	**CL**	P	*CR*	AL	58165	58365	58465	58265
168 216	**CL**	P	*CR*	AL	58166	58366	58466	58266
168 217	**CL**	P	*CR*	AL	58167	58367	58467	58267
168 218	**CL**	P	*CR*	AL	58168		58468	58268
168 219	**CL**	P	*CR*	AL	58169		58469	58269

Class 168/3. Former South West Trains/TransPennine Express Class 170s taken on by Chiltern Railways in 2015–16 and renumbered in the 1683xx series. 170309 was originally numbered 170 399. DMSL(A)–DMSL(B).

50301–308/399. DMCL. Adtranz Derby 2000–01. –/59 1TD 2W. 45.8 t.
79301–308/399. DMSL. Adtranz Derby 2000–01. –/69 1T. 45.8 t.

168 321	(170 301)		**CL**	P	*CR*	AL	50301	79301
168 322	(170 302)		**CL**	P	*CR*	AL	50302	79302
168 323	(170 303)		**CL**	P	*CR*	AL	50303	79303
168 324	(170 304)		**CL**	P	*CR*	AL	50304	79304
168 325	(170 305)		**CL**	P	*CR*	AL	50305	79305
168 326	(170 306)		**CL**	P	*CR*	AL	50306	79306
168 327	(170 307)		**CL**	P	*CR*	AL	50307	79307
168 328	(170 308)		**CL**	P	*CR*	AL	50308	79308
168 329	(170 309)	*	**CL**	P	*CR*	AL	50399	79399

CLASS 170   TURBOSTAR ADTRANZ/BOMBARDIER

Various formations. Air conditioned.

Construction: Welded aluminium bodies with bolt-on steel ends.
Engines: One MTU 6R183TD13H of 315 kW (422 hp) at 1900 rpm.
Transmission: Hydraulic. Voith T211rzze to ZF final drive.
Bogies: One Adtranz P3–23 and one BREL T3–23 per car.
Couplers: BSI at outer ends (Dellner on 170/9), bar within later-build units.
Dimensions: 23.62/23.61 x 2.69 m.
Gangways: Within unit only.
Doors: Twin-leaf sliding plug.
Seating Layout: 1: 2+1 facing/unidirectional. 2: 2+2 unidirectional/facing.
Wheel Arrangement: 2-B (+ B-2) + B-2.
Maximum Speed: 100 mph.
Multiple Working: Within class and with Classes 150, 153, 155, 156, 158, 159 and 172.

Class 170/1. CrossCountry (former Midland Mainline) units. Lazareni seating. DMSL–MS–DMCL/DMSL–DMCL.

DMSL. Adtranz Derby 1998–99. –/59 1TD 2W. 45.0 t.
MS. Adtranz Derby 2001. –/80. 43.0 t.
DMCL. Adtranz Derby 1998–99. 9/52 1T. 44.8 t

170 101	**XC**	P	*XC*	TS	50101	55101	79101
170 102	**XC**	P	*XC*	TS	50102	55102	79102
170 103	**XC**	P	*XC*	TS	50103	55103	79103
170 104	**XC**	P	*XC*	TS	50104	55104	79104
170 105	**XC**	P	*XC*	TS	50105	55105	79105
170 106	**XC**	P	*XC*	TS	50106	55106	79106
170 107	**XC**	P	*XC*	TS	50107	55107	79107
170 108	**XC**	P	*XC*	TS	50108	55108	79108
170 109	**XC**	P	*XC*	TS	50109	55109	79109
170 110	**XC**	P	*XC*	TS	50110	55110	79110
170 111	**XC**	P	*XC*	TS	50111		79111
170 112	**XC**	P	*XC*	TS	50112		79112
170 113	**XC**	P	*XC*	TS	50113		79113
170 114	**XC**	P	*XC*	TS	50114		79114
170 115	**XC**	P	*XC*	TS	50115		79115
170 116	**XC**	P	*XC*	TS	50116		79116
170 117	**XC**	P	*XC*	TS	50117		79117

Class 170/2. East Midlands Railway and Transport for Wales 3-car units. Previously operated by Greater Anglia. 170 206–208 due to transfer to East Midlands Railway late 2023. Chapman seating. DMCL–MSL–DMSL.

DMCL. Adtranz Derby 1999. 7/39 1TD 2W. 44.3 t.
MSL. Adtranz Derby 1999. –/74 1T. 42.8 t.
DMSL. Adtranz Derby 1999. –/66 1T. 44.8 t.

170 201	**ER**	P	*EM*	DY	50201	56201	79201
170 202	**ER**	P	*EM*	DY	50202	56202	79202
170 203	**ER**	P	*EM*	DY	50203	56203	79203
170 204	**ER**	P	*EM*	DY	50204	56204	79204
170 205	**ER**	P	*EM*	DY	50205	56205	79205

170 206	**GA**	P	*TW*	CF	50206	56206	79206
170 207	**GA**	P	*TW*	CF	50207	56207	79207
170 208	**GA**	P	*TW*	CF	50208	56208	79208

Class 170/2. East Midlands Railway 2-car units. Previously operated by Greater Anglia and Transport for Wales. Chapman seating. DMSL–DMCL.

DMSL. Bombardier Derby 2002. –/57 1TD 2W. 45.7 t.
DMCL. Bombardier Derby 2002. 9/53 1T. 45.7 t.

170 270	**ER**	P	*EM*	DY	50270	79270
170 271	**ER**	P	*EM*	DY	50271	79271
170 272	**ER**	P	*EM*	DY	50272	79272
170 273	**ER**	P	*EM*	DY	50273	79273

Class 170/3. Units built for Hull Trains, now used by ScotRail. Chapman seating. DMSL–MSL–DMSL.

DMSL(A). Bombardier Derby 2004. –/55 1TD 2W. 46.5 t.
MSL. Bombardier Derby 2004. –/71 1T. 44.7 t.
DMSL(B). Bombardier Derby 2004. –/67 1T. 47.0 t.

170 393	**SR**	P	*SR*	HA	50393	56393	79393
170 394	**SR**	P	*SR*	HA	50394	56394	79394
170 395	**SR**	P	*SR*	HA	50395	56395	79395
170 396	**SR**	P	*SR*	HA	50396	56396	79396

Class 170/3. CrossCountry units. Lazareni seating. DMSL–MS–DMCL.

DMSL. Bombardier Derby 2002. –/59 1TD 2W. 45.4 t.
MS. Bombardier Derby 2002. –/80. 43.0 t.
DMCL. Bombardier Derby 2002. 9/52 1T. 45.8 t.

| 170 397 | **XC** | P | *XC* | TS | 50397 | 56397 | 79397 |
| 170 398 | **XC** | P | *XC* | TS | 50398 | 56398 | 79398 |

Class 170/4. ScotRail and East Midlands Railway units. Chapman seating. DMCL–MS–DMCL.

170422–424 were numbered 170922–924 in 2022–23. Originally ex-Scotland and latterly ex-Southern 171 201/202 and 171 401/402.

Advertising livery: 170 407 BTP text number 61016 (blue).

DMCL(A). Adtranz Derby 1999–2001. 9/43 1TD 2W. 45.2 t.
MS. Adtranz Derby 1999–2001. –/76. 42.5 t.
DMCL(B). Adtranz Derby 1999–2001. 9/49 1T. 45.2 t.

170 401	**SR**	P	*SR*	HA	50401	56401	79401
170 402	**SR**	P	*SR*	HA	50402	56402	79402
170 403	**SR**	P	*SR*	HA	50403	56403	79403
170 404	**SR**	P	*SR*	HA	50404	56404	79404
170 405	**SR**	P	*SR*	HA	50405	56405	79405
170 406	**SR**	P	*SR*	HA	50406	56406	79406
170 407	**AL**	P	*SR*	HA	50407	56407	79407
170 408	**SR**	P	*SR*	HA	50408	56408	79408
170 409	**SR**	P	*SR*	HA	50409	56409	79409
170 410	**SR**	P	*SR*	HA	50410	56410	79410

170 411	**SR**	P	*SR*	HA	50411	56411	79411	
170 412	**SR**	P	*SR*	HA	50412	56412	79412	
170 413	**SR**	P	*SR*	HA	50413	56413	79413	
170 414	**SR**	P	*SR*	HA	50414	56414	79414	
170 415	**SR**	P	*SR*	HA	50415	56415	79415	
170 416	**ER**	E	*EM*	DY	50416	56416	79416	
170 417	**ER**	E	*EM*	DY	50417	56417	79417	The Key Worker
170 418	**ER**	E	*EM*	DY	50418	56418	79418	
170 419	**ER**	E	*EM*	DY	50419	56419	79419	
170 420	**ER**	E	*EM*	DY	50420	56420	79420	
170 422	**SN**	E	*EM*	DY	50422	56422	79422	
170 423	**SN**	E	*EM*	DY	50423	56423	79423	
170 424	**SN**	E	*EM*	DY	50424	56424	79424	

Class 170/4. ScotRail units. Chapman seating. DMCL–MS–DMCL.

DMCL. Bombardier Derby 2003–05. 9/43 1TD 2W. 46.8 t.
MS. Bombardier Derby 2003–05. –/76. 43.7 t.
DMCL. Bombardier Derby 2003–05. 9/49 1T. 46.5 t.

170 425	**SR**	P	*SR*	HA	50425	56425	79425
170 426	**SR**	P	*SR*	HA	50426	56426	79426
170 427	**SR**	P	*SR*	HA	50427	56427	79427
170 428	**SR**	P	*SR*	HA	50428	56428	79428
170 429	**SR**	P	*SR*	HA	50429	56429	79429
170 430	**SR**	P	*SR*	HA	50430	56430	79430
170 431	**SR**	P	*SR*	HA	50431	56431	79431
170 432	**SR**	P	*SR*	HA	50432	56432	79432
170 433	**SR**	P	*SR*	HA	50433	56433	79433
170 434	**SR**	P	*SR*	HA	50434	56434	79434

Class 170/4. ScotRail and Northern units. Originally built as Standard Class only. 170450–457 were retro-fitted with First Class but those used by Northern are now Standard Class only. Chapman seating. DMSL–MS–DMSL or † DMCL–MS–DMCL.

DMSL/DMCL. Bombardier Derby 2004–05. –/55 1TD 2W († 9/47 1TD 2W). 46.3 t.
MS. Bombardier Derby 2004–05. –/76. 43.4 t.
DMSL/DMCL. Bombardier Derby 2004–05. –/67 1T († 9/49 1T 1W). 46.4 t.

170 450	†	**SR**	P	*SR*	HA	50450	56450	79450
170 451	†	**SR**	P	*SR*	HA	50451	56451	79451
170 452	†	**SR**	P	*SR*	HA	50452	56452	79452
170 453	†	**NR**	P	*NO*	BG	50453	56453	79453
170 454	†	**NR**	P	*NO*	BG	50454	56454	79454
170 455	†	**NR**	P	*NO*	BG	50455	56455	79455
170 456	†	**NR**	P	*NO*	BG	50456	56456	79456
170 457	†	**NR**	P	*NO*	BG	50457	56457	79457
170 458		**NR**	P	*NO*	BG	50458	56458	79458
170 459		**NR**	P	*NO*	BG	50459	56459	79459
170 460		**NR**	P	*NO*	BG	50460	56460	79460
170 461		**NR**	P	*NO*	BG	50461	56461	79461

Class 170/4. ScotRail and Northern units. Standard Class only units. Chapman seating. DMSL–MS–DMSL.

50470–471. DMSL(A). Adtranz Derby 2001. –/55 1TD 2W. 45.1 t.
50472–478. DMSL(A). Bombardier Derby 2004–05. –/57 1TD 2W. 45.8 t.
56470–471. MS. Adtranz Derby 2001. –/76. 42.4 t.
56472–478. MS. Bombardier Derby 2004–05. –/76. 43.0 t.
79470–471. DMSL(B). Adtranz Derby 2001. –/67 1T. 45.1 t.
79472–478. DMSL(B). Bombardier Derby 2004–05. –/67 1T. 45.8 t.

170 470	**SR**	P	*SR*	HA	50470	56470	79470
170 471	**SR**	P	*SR*	HA	50471	56471	79471
170 472	**NR**	P	*NO*	BG	50472	56472	79472
170 473	**NR**	P	*NO*	BG	50473	56473	79473
170 474	**NR**	P	*NO*	BG	50474	56474	79474
170 475	**NR**	P	*NO*	BG	50475	56475	79475
170 476	**NR**	P	*NO*	BG	50476	56476	79476
170 477	**NR**	P	*NO*	BG	50477	56477	79477
170 478	**NR**	P	*NO*	BG	50478	56478	79478

Class 170/5. East Midlands Railway 2-car units. Lazareni seating. DMSL–DMSL.

170530–535 were reduced from 3-car units to 2-car units in 2020 prior to their transfer (along with 170501–517) to East Midlands Railway.

DMSL(A). Adtranz Derby 1999–2000. –/55 1TD 2W. 45.8 t.
DMSL(B). Adtranz Derby 1999–2000. –/67 1T. 45.9 t.

170 501	**ER**	P	*EM*	DY	50501	79501	
170 502	**ER**	P	*EM*	DY	50502	79502	
170 503	**ER**	P	*EM*	DY	50503	79503	
170 504	**ER**	P	*EM*	DY	50504	79504	
170 505	**ER**	P	*EM*	DY	50505	79505	
170 506	**ER**	P	*EM*	DY	50506	79506	
170 507	**ER**	P	*EM*	DY	50507	79507	
170 508	**ER**	P	*EM*	DY	50508	79508	
170 509	**ER**	P	*EM*	DY	50509	79509	
170 510	**ER**	P	*EM*	DY	50510	79510	
170 511	**ER**	P	*EM*	DY	50511	79511	
170 512	**ER**	P	*EM*	DY	50512	79512	
170 513	**ER**	P	*EM*	DY	50513	79513	
170 514	**ER**	P	*EM*	DY	50514	79514	
170 515	**ER**	P	*EM*	DY	50515	79515	
170 516	**ER**	P	*EM*	DY	50516	79516	
170 517	**ER**	P	*EM*	DY	50517	79517	
170 530	(170 630)	**ER**	P	*EM*	DY	50630	79630
170 531	(170 631)	**ER**	P	*EM*	DY	50631	79631
170 532	(170 632)	**ER**	P	*EM*	DY	50632	79632
170 533	(170 633)	**ER**	P	*EM*	DY	50633	79633
170 534	(170 634)	**ER**	P	*EM*	DY	50634	79634
170 535	(170 635)	**ER**	P	*EM*	DY	50635	79635

Class 170/6. CrossCountry 3-car units. Lazareni seating. DMSL–MS–DMCL.

170 618–623 were augmented from 2-car to 3-car in 2020–21 using centre cars from 170 630–635, having been built as 2-car units 170 518–523.

DMSL. Adtranz Derby 2000. –/59 1TD 2W. 45.8 t.
MS. Adtranz Derby 2000. –/74. 42.5 t.
DMCL. Adtranz Derby 2000. 9/52 1T. 45.9 t.

170 618	(170 518)	**XC**	P	*XC*	TS	50518	56630	79518
170 619	(170 519)	**XC**	P	*XC*	TS	50519	56631	79519
170 620	(170 520)	**XC**	P	*XC*	TS	50520	56632	79520
170 621	(170 521)	**XC**	P	*XC*	TS	50521	56633	79521
170 622	(170 522)	**XC**	P	*XC*	TS	50522	56634	79522
170 623	(170 523)	**XC**	P	*XC*	TS	50523	56635	79523

170 636	**XC**	P	*XC*	TS	50636	56636	79636
170 637	**XC**	P	*XC*	TS	50637	56637	79637
170 638	**XC**	P	*XC*	TS	50638	56638	79638
170 639	**XC**	P	*XC*	TS	50639	56639	79639

Name (carried on MS): 170 622   PRIDE OF LEICESTER

CLASS 171   TURBOSTAR   BOMBARDIER

DMCL–DMSL or DMCL–MS–DMCL. Southern units. Air conditioned. Chapman seating.

Construction: Welded aluminium bodies with bolt-on steel ends.
Engines: One MTU 6R183TD13H of 315 kW (422 hp) at 1900 rpm.
Transmission: Hydraulic. Voith T211rzze to ZF final drive.
Bogies: One Adtranz P3–23 and one BREL T3–23 per car.
Couplers: Dellner 12 at outer ends, bar within unit (Class 171/8).
Dimensions: 23.62/23.61 x 2.69 m.
Gangways: Within unit only.   **Wheel Arrangement:** 2-B (+ B-2 + B-2) + B-2.
Doors: Twin-leaf swing plug.   **Maximum Speed:** 100 mph.
Seating Layout: 1: 2+1 facing/unidirectional. 2: 2+2 facing/unidirectional.
Multiple Working: Within class and with EMU Classes 375 and 377 in an emergency.

Class 171/2. 3-car unit rebuilt from ScotRail Class 170. DMCL–MS–DMCL. On short-term hire from East Midlands Railway to Southern.

DMCL(A). Adtranz Derby 1999–2001. 9/43 1TD 2W. 45.2 t.
MS. Adtranz Derby 1999–2001. –/76. 42.5 t.
DMCL(B). Adtranz Derby 1999–2001. 9/49 1T. 45.2 t.

171 201	(170 421)	**SN**	P	*SN*	SU	50421	56421	79421

Class 171/7. 2-car units. DMCL–DMSL.

171 730 was formerly South West Trains unit 170 392, before transferring to Southern in 2007.

50727–729. DMCL. Bombardier Derby 2005. 9/43 1TD 2W. 46.3 t.
50392. DMCL. Bombardier Derby 2003. 9/43 1TD 2W. 46.6 t.

79727–729. DMSL. Bombardier Derby 2005. –/64 1T. 46.2 t.
79392. DMSL. Bombardier Derby 2003. –/64 1T. 46.5 t.

171 727	**SN**	P	*SN*	SU	50727	79727
171 728	**SN**	P	*SN*	SU	50728	79728
171 729	**SN**	P	*SN*	SU	50729	79729
171 730	**SN**	P	*SN*	SU	50392	79392

Class 171/8. Built as 4-car units but reduced to 3-car units in 2022. DMCL(A)–MS–DMCL(B).

DMCL(A). Bombardier Derby 2004. 9/43 1TD 2W. 46.5 t.
MS. Bombardier Derby 2004. –/74. 43.7 t.
DMCL(B). Bombardier Derby 2004. 9/50 1T. 46.5 t.

171 801	**SN**	P	*SN*	SU	50801	54801	79801
171 802	**SN**	P	*SN*	SU	50802	54802	79802
171 803	**SN**	P	*SN*	SU	50803	54803	79803
171 804	**SN**	P	*SN*	SU	50804	54804	79804
171 805	**SN**	P	*SN*	SU	50805	54805	79805
171 806	**SN**	P	*SN*	SU	50806	54806	79806

Class 171/8. Former 2-car units extended to 3-car units in 2022 using MS vehicles from 171 801–806. DMCL–MS–DMSL.

DMCL. Bombardier Derby 2003. 9/43 1TD 2W. 47.6 t.
MS. Bombardier Derby 2004. –/74. 43.7 t.
DMSL. Bombardier Derby 2003. –/64 1T. 47.8 t.

171 807	(171 721)	**SN**	P	*SN*	SU	50721	56806	79721
171 808	(171 722)	**SN**	P	*SN*	SU	50722	56804	79722
171 809	(171 723)	**SN**	P	*SN*	SU	50723	56802	79723
171 810	(171 724)	**SN**	P	*SN*	SU	50724	56805	79724
171 811	(171 725)	**SN**	P	*SN*	SU	50725	56803	79725
171 812	(171 726)	**SN**	P	*SN*	SU	50726	56801	79726

CLASS 172   TURBOSTAR   BOMBARDIER

New generation West Midlands Trains Turbostars. Air conditioned.

Construction: Welded aluminium bodies with bolt-on steel ends.
Engines: One MTU 6H1800R83 of 360 kW (483 hp) at 1800 rpm.
Transmission: Mechanical. Supplied by ZF, Germany.
Bogies: B5006 type "lightweight" bogies.
Couplers: BSI at outer ends, bar within unit.
Dimensions: 23.62/23.00 x 2.69 m.
Gangways: 172/0 & 172/1: Within unit only. 172/2: Throughout.
Wheel Arrangement: 2-B (+ B-2) + B-2.
Doors: Twin-leaf sliding plug.
Maximum Speed: 100 mph.
Seating Layout: 2+2 facing/unidirectional.
Multiple Working: Within class and with Classes 150, 153, 155, 156, 158, 159, 165, 166 and 170.

Class 172/0. Formerly operated by London Overground. DMSL–DMS.

59311–318. DMSL. Bombardier Derby 2009–10. –/57(+4) 1TD 2W. 41.6 t.
59411–418. DMS. Bombardier Derby 2009–10. –/64(+12). 41.5 t.

172 001	WM	A	WM	TS	59311	59411
172 002	WM	A	WM	TS	59312	59412
172 003	WM	A	WM	TS	59313	59413
172 004	WM	A	WM	TS	59314	59414
172 005	WM	A	WM	TS	59315	59415
172 006	WM	A	WM	TS	59316	59416
172 007	WM	A	WM	TS	59317	59417
172 008	WM	A	WM	TS	59318	59418

Class 172/1. Formerly operated by Chiltern Railways. DMSL–DMS.

59111–114. DMSL. Bombardier Derby 2009–10. –/60(+5) 1TD 2W. 42.4 t.
59211–214. DMS. Bombardier Derby 2009–10. –/80. 41.8 t.

172 101	WM	A	WM	TS	59111	59211
172 102	WM	A	WM	TS	59112	59212
172 103	WM	A	WM	TS	59113	59213
172 104	WM	A	WM	TS	59114	59214

Class 172/2. 2-car units with end gangways. DMSL–DMS.

50211–222. DMSL. Bombardier Derby 2010–11. –/52(+11) 1TD 2W. 42.5 t.
79211–222. DMS. Bombardier Derby 2010–11. –/68(+8). 41.9 t.

172 211	WM	P	WM	TS	50211	79211
172 212	WM	P	WM	TS	50212	79212
172 213	WM	P	WM	TS	50213	79213
172 214	WM	P	WM	TS	50214	79214
172 215	WM	P	WM	TS	50215	79215
172 216	WM	P	WM	TS	50216	79216
172 217	WM	P	WM	TS	50217	79217
172 218	WM	P	WM	TS	50218	79218
172 219	WM	P	WM	TS	50219	79219
172 220	WM	P	WM	TS	50220	79220
172 221	WM	P	WM	TS	50221	79221
172 222	WM	P	WM	TS	50222	79222

Class 172/3. 3-car units with end gangways. DMSL–MS–DMS.

172 333/338 are running with misformed formations, as shown.

50331–345. DMSL. Bombardier Derby 2010–11. –/52(+11) 1TD 2W. 42.5 t.
56331–345. MS. Bombardier Derby 2010–11. –/72(+8). 38.8 t.
79331–345. DMS. Bombardier Derby 2010–11. –/68(+8). 41.9 t.

172 331	WM	P	WM	TS	50331	56331	79331
172 332	WM	P	WM	TS	50332	56332	79332
172 333	WM	P	WM	TS	50338	56333	79333
172 334	WM	P	WM	TS	50334	56334	79334
172 335	WM	P	WM	TS	50335	56335	79335
172 336	WM	P	WM	TS	50336	56336	79336
172 337	WM	P	WM	TS	50337	56337	79337

172 338	**WM** P	*WM*	TS	50333	56338	79338	
172 339	**WM** P	*WM*	TS	50339	56339	79339	
172 340	**WM** P	*WM*	TS	50340	56340	79340	
172 341	**WM** P	*WM*	TS	50341	56341	79341	
172 342	**WM** P	*WM*	TS	50342	56342	79342	ROGER SUMNER
172 343	**WM** P	*WM*	TS	50343	56343	79343	
172 344	**WM** P	*WM*	TS	50344	56344	79344	
172 345	**WM** P	*WM*	TS	50345	56345	79345	

CLASS 175   CORADIA 1000   ALSTOM

Air conditioned.

Construction: Steel.
Engines: One Cummins N14 of 335 kW (450 hp).
Transmission: Hydraulic. Voith T211rzze to ZF Voith final drive.
Bogies: ACR (Alstom FBO) – LTB-MBS1, TB-MB1, MBS1-LTB.
Couplers: Scharfenberg outer ends and bar within unit (Class 175/1).
Dimensions: 23.70 x 2.73 m.
Gangways: Within unit only.   **Wheel Arrangement:** 2-B (+ B-2) + B-2.
Doors: Single-leaf swing plug.   **Maximum Speed:** 100 mph.
Seating Layout: 2+2 facing/unidirectional.
Multiple Working: Within class and with Class 180.

All units due to be withdrawn by the end of 2023.

175 004/005/006/101/109/115 are in misformed formations, as shown.

Class 175/0. DMSL–DMSL. 2-car units.

DMSL(A). Alstom Birmingham 1999–2000. –/54 1TD 2W. 48.8 t.
DMSL(B). Alstom Birmingham 1999–2000. –/64 1T. 50.7 t.

175 001	**TW** A	ZI	50701	79701
175 002	**TW** A	LE	50702	79702
175 003	**TW** A	HD	50703	79703
175 004	**TW** A	LE	50759	79759
175 005	**TW** A	ZI	50705	79751
175 006	**TW** A	LE	50706	79765
175 007	**TW** A	LE	50707	79707
175 008	**TW** A	ZI	50708	79708
175 009	**TW** A	ZI	50709	79709
175 010	**TW** A	ZI	50710	79710
175 011	**TW** Λ	CY	50711	79711

Class 175/1. DMSL–MSL–DMSL. 3-car units.

DMSL(A). Alstom Birmingham 1999–2001. –/54 1TD 2W. 50.7 t.
MSL. Alstom Birmingham 1999–2001. –/68 1T. 47.5 t.
DMSL(B). Alstom Birmingham 1999–2001. –/64 1T. 49.5 t.

175 101	**TW** A	*TW*	CH	50751	56751	79704
175 102	**TW** A		LE	50752	56752	79752

175 103	**TW**	A		HD	50753	56753	79753
175 104	**TW**	A		HD	50754	56754	79754
175 105	**TW**	A		CY	50755	56755	79755
175 106	**TW**	A		HD	50756	56756	79756
175 107	**TW**	A		CY	50757	56757	79757
175 108	**TW**	A		CH	50758	56758	79758
175 109	**TW**	A	*TW*	CH	50704	56759	79705
175 110	**TW**	A		CF	50760	56760	79760
175 111	**TW**	A		MA	50761	56761	79761
175 112	**TW**	A		HD	50762	56762	79762
175 113	**TW**	A	*TW*	CH	50763	56763	79763
175 114	**TW**	A	*TW*	CH	50764	56764	79764
175 115	**TW**	A	*TW*	CH	50765	56765	79706
175 116	**TW**	A		LE	50766	56766	79766

CLASS 180   CORADIA 1000   ALSTOM

Air conditioned.

Construction: Steel.
Engines: One Cummins QSK19 of 560 kW (750 hp) at 2100 rpm.
Transmission: Hydraulic. Voith T312br to Voith final drive.
Bogies: ACR (Alstom FBO): LTB1-MBS2, TB1-MB2, TB1-MB2, TB2-MB2, MBS2-LTB1.
Couplers: Scharfenberg outer ends, bar within unit.
Dimensions: 23.71/23.03 x 2.73 m.
Gangways: Within unit only.
Wheel Arrangement: 2-B + B-2 + B-2 + B-2 + B-2.
Doors: Single-leaf swing plug.   **Maximum Speed:** 125 mph.
Seating Layout: 1: 2+1 facing/unidirectional, 2: 2+2 facing/unidirectional.
Multiple Working: Within class and with Class 175.

A number of Grand Central Class 180 sets are currently running with misformed formations, as shown. Set 180 103 is having repairs undertaken.

DMSL(A). Alstom Birmingham 2000–01. –/46 2W 1TD. 51.7 t.
MFL. Alstom Birmingham 2000–01. 42/– 1T 1W + catering point. 49.6 t.
MSL. Alstom Birmingham 2000–01. –/68 1T. 49.5 t.
MSLRB. Alstom Birmingham 2000–01. –/56 1T. 50.3 t.
DMSL(B). Alstom Birmingham 2000–01. –/56 1T. 51.4 t.

180 101	**GC**	A	*GC*	HT	50901	54901	55901	56901	59903
180 102	**GC**	A	*GC*	HT	50902	54902	55902	56902	59902
180 103	**GC**	A	*GC*	HT	50912	54907	55906	56903	59905
180 104	**GC**	A	*GC*	HT	50904	54904	55904	56904	59904
180 105	**GC**	A	*GC*	HT	50905	54905	55905	56905	59901
180 106	**GC**	A	*GC*	HT	50906	54906	55903	56906	59906
180 107	**GC**	A	*GC*	HT	50907	54903	55907	56907	59907
180 108	**GC**	A	*GC*	HT	50908	54908	55908	56908	59908
180 109	**EI**	A		EP	50909	54909	55909	56909	59909
180 110	**EI**	A	*GC*	HT	50910	54910	55910	56910	59910
180 111	**EI**	A		EP	50911	54911	55911	56911	59911

180 112	**GC**	A	*GC*	HT	50903 54912 55912 56912 59912
180 113	**El**	A		EP	50913 54913 55913 56913 59913
180 114	**GC**	A	*GC*	HT	50914 54914 55914 56914 59914

Names (carried on DMSL(A))

180 105	THE YORKSHIRE ARTIST ASHLEY JACKSON
180 107	HART OF THE NORTH
180 108	WILLIAM SHAKESPEARE
180 112	JAMES HERRIOT
180 114	KIRKGATE CALLING

CLASS 185   DESIRO UK   SIEMENS

Air conditioned. Grammer seating in Standard Class and Fainsa in First Class.

Construction: Aluminium.
Engines: One Cummins QSK19 of 560 kW (750 hp) at 2100 rpm.
Transmission: Voith.   **Bogies:** Siemens.
Couplers: Dellner 12.   **Dimensions:** 23.76/23.75 x 2.66 m.
Gangways: Within unit only.   **Wheel Arrangement:** 2-B + 2-B + B-2.
Doors: Double-leaf sliding plug.   **Maximum Speed:** 100 mph.
Seating Layout: 1: 2+1 facing/unidirectional, 2: 2+2 facing/unidirectional.
Multiple Working: Within class only.

DMCL. Siemens Krefeld 2005–06. 15/18(+8) 2W 1TD + catering point. 55.4 t.
MSL. Siemens Krefeld 2005–06. –/72 1T. 52.7 t.
DMS. Siemens Krefeld 2005–06. –/64(+4). 54.9 t.

185 101	**TP**	E	*TP*	AK	51101 53101 54101
185 102	**TP**	E	*TP*	AK	51102 53102 54102
185 103	**TP**	E	*TP*	AK	51103 53103 54103
185 104	**TP**	E	*TP*	AK	51104 53104 54104
185 105	**TP**	E	*TP*	AK	51105 53105 54105
185 106	**TP**	E	*TP*	AK	51106 53106 54106
185 107	**TP**	E	*TP*	AK	51107 53107 54107
185 108	**TP**	E	*TP*	AK	51108 53108 54108
185 109	**TP**	E	*TP*	AK	51109 53109 54109
185 110	**TP**	E	*TP*	AK	51110 53110 54110
185 111	**TP**	E	*TP*	AK	51111 53111 54111
185 112	**TP**	E	*TP*	AK	51112 53112 54112
185 113	**TP**	E	*TP*	AK	51113 53113 54113
185 114	**TP**	E	*TP*	AK	51114 53114 54114
185 115	**TP**	E	*TP*	AK	51115 53115 54115
185 116	**TP**	E	*TP*	AK	51116 53116 54116
185 117	**TP**	E	*TP*	AK	51117 53117 54117
185 118	**TP**	E	*TP*	AK	51118 53118 54118
185 119	**TP**	E	*TP*	AK	51119 53119 54119
185 120	**TP**	E	*TP*	AK	51120 53120 54120
185 121	**TP**	E	*TP*	AK	51121 53121 54121
185 122	**TP**	E	*TP*	AK	51122 53122 54122
185 123	**TP**	E	*TP*	AK	51123 53123 54123
185 124	**TP**	E	*TP*	AK	51124 53124 54124

185 125	**TP**	E	*TP*	AK	51125	53125	54125
185 126	**TP**	E	*TP*	AK	51126	53126	54126
185 127	**TP**	E	*TP*	AK	51127	53127	54127
185 128	**TP**	E	*TP*	AK	51128	53128	54128
185 129	**TP**	E	*TP*	AK	51129	53129	54129
185 130	**TP**	E	*TP*	AK	51130	53130	54130
185 131	**TP**	E	*TP*	AK	51131	53131	54131
185 132	**TP**	E	*TP*	AK	51132	53132	54132
185 133	**TP**	E	*TP*	AK	51133	53133	54133
185 134	**TP**	E	*TP*	AK	51134	53134	54134
185 135	**TP**	E	*TP*	AK	51135	53135	54135
185 136	**TP**	E	*TP*	AK	51136	53136	54136
185 137	**TP**	E	*TP*	AK	51137	53137	54137
185 138	**TP**	E	*TP*	AK	51138	53138	54138
185 139	**TP**	E	*TP*	AK	51139	53139	54139
185 140	**TP**	E	*TP*	AK	51140	53140	54140
185 141	**TP**	E	*TP*	AK	51141	53141	54141
185 142	**TP**	E	*TP*	AK	51142	53142	54142
185 143	**TP**	E	*TP*	AK	51143	53143	54143
185 144	**TP**	E	*TP*	AK	51144	53144	54144
185 145	**TP**	E	*TP*	AK	51145	53145	54145
185 146	**TP**	E	*TP*	AK	51146	53146	54146
185 147	**TP**	E	*TP*	AK	51147	53147	54147
185 148	**TP**	E	*TP*	AK	51148	53148	54148
185 149	**TP**	E	*TP*	AK	51149	53149	54149
185 150	**TP**	E	*TP*	AK	51150	53150	54150
185 151	**TP**	E	*TP*	AK	51151	53151	54151

CLASS 195   CIVITY   CAF

DMS–DMS or DMS–MS–DMS. New Northern units. Air conditioned.

Construction: Aluminium.
Engines: One Rolls-Royce MTU 6H 1800 R85L of 390 kW (523 hp) per car.
Transmission: Mechanical, supplied by ZF, Germany.
Bogies: CAF.
Couplers: Dellner 12.   **Dimensions:** 24.03/23.35 x 2.71 m.
Gangways: Within unit only.   **Wheel Arrangement:**
Doors: Sliding plug.   **Maximum Speed:** 100 mph.
Seating Layout: 2+2 facing/unidirectional.
Multiple Working: Within class only.

Class 195/0. DMS–DMS. 2-car units.

DMS(A). CAF Zaragoza/Irun/Newport 2017–20. –/45(+8) 1TD 2W. 43.9 t.
DMS(B). CAF Zaragoza/Irun/Newport 2017–20. –/63(+7). 43.2 t.

195 001	**NR**	E	*NO*	NH	101001	103001
195 002	**NR**	E	*NO*	NH	101002	103002
195 003	**NR**	E	*NO*	NH	101003	103003
195 004	**NR**	E	*NO*	NH	101004	103004
195 005	**NR**	E	*NO*	NH	101005	103005
195 006	**NR**	E	*NO*	NH	101006	103006

195 007	**NR**	E	*NO*	NH	101007	103007	
195 008	**NR**	E	*NO*	NH	101008	103008	
195 009	**NR**	E	*NO*	NH	101009	103009	
195 010	**NR**	E	*NO*	NH	101010	103010	
195 011	**NR**	E	*NO*	NH	101011	103011	
195 012	**NR**	E	*NO*	NH	101012	103012	
195 013	**NR**	E	*NO*	NH	101013	103013	
195 014	**NR**	E	*NO*	NH	101014	103014	
195 015	**NR**	E	*NO*	NH	101015	103015	
195 016	**NR**	E	*NO*	NH	101016	103016	
195 017	**NR**	E	*NO*	NH	101017	103017	
195 018	**NR**	E	*NO*	NH	101018	103018	
195 019	**NR**	E	*NO*	NH	101019	103019	
195 020	**NR**	E	*NO*	NH	101020	103020	
195 021	**NR**	E	*NO*	NH	101021	103021	
195 022	**NR**	E	*NO*	NH	101022	103022	
195 023	**NR**	E	*NO*	NH	101023	103023	
195 024	**NR**	E	*NO*	NH	101024	103024	
195 025	**NR**	E	*NO*	NH	101025	103025	

Class 195/1. DMS–MS–DMS. 3-car units.

DMS(A). CAF Zaragoza/Irun/Newport 2017–20. –/45(+8) 1TD 2W. 43.9 t.
MS. CAF Zaragoza/Irun/Newport 2017–20. –/76(+4).
DMS(B). CAF Zaragoza/Irun/Newport 2017–20. –/63(+7). 43.2 t.

195 101	**NR**	E	*NO*	NH	101101	102101	103101	
195 102	**NR**	E	*NO*	NH	101102	102102	103102	
195 103	**NR**	E	*NO*	NH	101103	102103	103103	
195 104	**NR**	E	*NO*	NH	101104	102104	103104	Deva Victrix
195 105	**NR**	E	*NO*	NH	101105	102105	103105	
195 106	**NR**	E	*NO*	NH	101106	102106	103106	
195 107	**NR**	E	*NO*	NH	101107	102107	103107	
195 108	**NR**	E	*NO*	NH	101108	102108	103108	
195 109	**NR**	E	*NO*	NH	101109	102109	103109	Pride of Cumbria
195 110	**NR**	E	*NO*	NH	101110	102110	103110	
195 111	**NR**	E	*NO*	NH	101111	102111	103111	Key Worker
195 112	**NR**	E	*NO*	NH	101112	102112	103112	
195 113	**NR**	E	*NO*	NH	101113	102113	103113	
195 114	**NR**	E	*NO*	NH	101114	102114	103114	
195 115	**NR**	E	*NO*	NH	101115	102115	103115	
195 116	**NR**	E	*NO*	NH	101116	102116	103116	Proud to be Northern
195 117	**NR**	E	*NO*	NH	101117	102117	103117	
195 118	**NR**	E	*NO*	NH	101118	102118	103118	
195 119	**NR**	E	*NO*	NH	101119	102119	103119	
195 120	**NR**	E	*NO*	NH	101120	102120	103120	
195 121	**NR**	E	*NO*	NH	101121	102121	103121	
195 122	**NR**	E	*NO*	NH	101122	102122	103122	
195 123	**NR**	E	*NO*	NH	101123	102123	103123	
195 124	**NR**	E	*NO*	NH	101124	102124	103124	
195 125	**NR**	E	*NO*	NH	101125	102125	103125	
195 126	**NR**	E	*NO*	NH	101126	102126	103126	

195 127	**NR**	E	*NO*	NH	101127	102127	103127	
195 128	**NR**	E	*NO*	NH	101128	102128	103128	Calder Champion
195 129	**NR**	E	*NO*	NH	101129	102129	103129	
195 130	**NR**	E	*NO*	NH	101130	102130	103130	
195 131	**NR**	E	*NO*	NH	101131	102131	103131	
195 132	**NR**	E	*NO*	NH	101132	102132	103132	
195 133	**NR**	E	*NO*	NH	101133	102133	103133	

CLASS 196   CIVITY   CAF

DMS–DMS or DMS–MS–MS–DMS. New West Midlands Trains used on local services between Birmingham and Shrewsbury and Hereford. Air conditioned.

Construction: Aluminium.
Engines: One Rolls-Royce MTU 6H 1800 R85L of 390 kW (523 hp) per car.
Transmission: Mechanical, supplied by ZF, Germany.
Bogies: CAF.
Couplers: Dellner 12.   **Dimensions:** 24.03/23.35 x 2.71 m.
Gangways: Throughout.   **Wheel Arrangement:**
Doors: Sliding plug.   **Maximum Speed:** 100 mph.
Seating Layout: 2+2 facing/unidirectional.
Multiple Working: Within class only.

Class 196/0. DMS–DMS. 2-car units.

DMS(A). CAF Zaragoza/Beasain/Newport 2019–21. –/58(+4) 1TD 2W.
DMS(B). CAF Zaragoza/Beasain/Newport 2019–21. –/76(+3).

196 001	**WM**	CO	*WM*	TS	121001	124001	GRAISELEY WOLVES
196 002	**WM**	CO	*WM*	TS	121002	124002	
196 003	**WM**	CO	*WM*	TS	121003	124003	
196 004	**WM**	CO	*WM*	TS	121004	124004	SIR EDWARD ELGAR
196 005	**WM**	CO	*WM*	TS	121005	124005	
196 006	**WM**	CO	*WM*	TS	121006	124006	
196 007	**WM**	CO	*WM*	TS	121007	124007	
196 008	**WM**	CO	*WM*	TS	121008	124008	
196 009	**WM**	CO	*WM*	TS	121009	124009	
196 010	**WM**	CO	*WM*	TS	121010	124010	
196 011	**WM**	CO	*WM*	TS	121011	124011	
196 012	**WM**	CO	*WM*	TS	121012	124012	

Class 196/1. DMS–MS–MS–DMS. 4-car units.

DMS(A). CAF Zaragoza/Irun/Newport 2019–21. –/58(+4) 1TD 2W. 41.4 t.
MS(A). CAF Zaragoza/Irun/Newport 2019–21. –/88. 39.8 t.
MS(B). CAF Zaragoza/Irun/Newport 2019–21. –/82 1T. 40.3 t.
DMS(B). CAF Zaragoza/Irun/Newport 2019–21. –/76(+3). 42.7 t.

196 101	**WM**	CO	*WM*	TS	121101	122101	123101	124101
196 102	**WM**	CO	*WM*	TS	121102	122102	123102	124102
196 103	**WM**	CO	*WM*	TS	121103	122103	123103	124103
196 104	**WM**	CO	*WM*	TS	121104	122104	123104	124104
196 105	**WM**	CO	*WM*	TS	121105	122105	123105	124105

196 106	**WM** CO	*WM* TS	121106	122106	123106	124106
196 107	**WM** CO	*WM* TS	121107	122107	123107	124107
196 108	**WM** CO	*WM* TS	121108	122108	123108	124108
196 109	**WM** CO	*WM* TS	121109	122109	123109	124109
196 110	**WM** CO	*WM* TS	121110	122110	123110	124110
196 111	**WM** CO	*WM* TS	121111	122111	123111	124111
196 112	**WM** CO		121112	122112	123112	124112
196 113	**WM** CO		121113	122113	123113	124113
196 114	**WM** CO		121114	122114	123114	124114

Name (carried on end cars): 196 101   CHARLES DARWIN

CLASS 197   CIVITY   CAF

DMS–DMS or DMS–MS–DMS. New units currently entering service with Transport for Wales. Air conditioned.

21 2-car units will be fitted with ETCS signalling equipment for operating the Cambrian Lines (197003/022–041) and 14 3-car units (195 113–116) will also have First Class seating.

Construction: Aluminium.
Engines: One Rolls-Royce MTU 6H 1800 R85L of 390 kW (523 hp) per car.
Transmission: Mechanical, supplied by ZF, Germany.
Bogies: CAF.
Couplers: Dellner 12.   **Dimensions:** 24.03/23.35 x 2.71 m.
Gangways: Throughout.   **Wheel Arrangement:**
Doors: Sliding plug.   **Maximum Speed:** 100 mph.
Seating Layout: 2+2 facing/unidirectional.
Multiple Working: Within class only.

Class 197/0. DMS–DMS. 2-car units.

DMS(A). CAF Beasain/Newport 2020–23. –/42(+6) 1TD 2W + catering area.
DMS(B). CAF Beasain/Newport 2020–23. –/74.

197 001	**TW** SM	*TW* CH	131001	133001	
197 002	**TW** SM	*TW* CH	131002	133002	
197 003	**TW** SM		131003	133003	
197 004	**TW** SM	*TW* CH	131004	133004	
197 005	**TW** SM		131005	133005	
197 006	**TW** SM	*TW* CH	131006	133006	
197 007	**TW** SM	*TW* CH	131007	133007	Happy Valley
197 008	**TW** SM	*TW* CH	131008	133008	
197 009	**TW** SM	*TW* CH	131009	133009	
197 010	**TW** SM	*TW* CH	131010	133010	
197 011	**TW** SM	*TW* CH	131011	133011	
197 012	**TW** SM	*TW* CH	131012	133012	
197 013	**TW** SM	*TW* CH	131013	133013	
197 014	**TW** SM	*TW* CH	131014	133014	
197 015	**TW** SM	*TW* CH	131015	133015	
197 016	**TW** SM	*TW* CH	131016	133016	
197 017	**TW** SM	*TW* CH	131017	133017	
197 018	**TW** SM	*TW* CH	131018	133018	

197 019	**TW**	SM	*TW*	CH	131019	133019
197 020	**TW**	SM	*TW*	CH	131020	133020
197 021	**TW**	SM	*TW*	CH	131021	133021
197 022	**TW**	SM			131022	133022
197 023	**TW**	SM			131023	133023
197 024	**TW**	SM			131024	133024
197 025	**TW**	SM			131025	133025
197 026	**TW**	SM			131026	133026
197 027	**TW**	SM			131027	133027
197 028	**TW**	SM			131028	133028
197 029	**TW**	SM			131029	133029
197 030	**TW**	SM			131030	133030
197 031	**TW**	SM			131031	133031
197 032	**TW**	SM			131032	133032
197 033	**TW**	SM			131033	133033
197 034	**TW**	SM			131034	133034
197 035	**TW**	SM			131035	133035
197 036	**TW**	SM			131036	133036
197 037	**TW**	SM			131037	133037
197 038	**TW**	SM			131038	133038
197 039	**TW**	SM			131039	133039
197 040	**TW**	SM			131040	133040
197 041	**TW**	SM			131041	133041
197 042	**TW**	SM	*TW*	CH	131042	133042
197 043	**TW**	SM	*TW*	CH	131043	133043
197 044	**TW**	SM	*TW*	CH	131044	133044
197 045	**TW**	SM			131045	133045
197 046	**TW**	SM	*TW*	CH	131046	133046
197 047	**TW**	SM	*TW*	CH	131047	133047
197 048	**TW**	SM	*TW*	CH	131048	133048
197 049	**TW**	SM	*TW*	CH	131049	133049
197 050	**TW**	SM			131050	133050
197 051	**TW**	SM	*TW*	CH	131051	133051

Class 197/1. DMS–MS–DMS or DMS–MS–DMC. 3-car units.

DMS(A). CAF Beasain/Newport 2020–23. –/42(+6) 1TD 2W + catering area.
MS. CAF Beasain/Newport 2020–23. –/72(+3) 1T.
DMS(B). CAF Beasain/Newport 2020–23. –/74 (* DMC 16/42).

197 101	**TW**	SM	*TW*	CH	131101	132101	133101
197 102	**TW**	SM			131102	132102	133102
197 103	**TW**	SM			131103	132103	133103
197 104	**TW**	SM	*TW*	CH	131104	132104	133104
197 105	**TW**	SM	*TW*	CH	131105	132105	133105
197 106	**TW**	SM			131106	132106	133106
197 107	**TW**	SM			131107	132107	133107
197 108	**TW**	SM			131108	132108	133108
197 109	**TW**	SM			131109	132109	133109
197 110	**TW**	SM	*TW*	CH	131110	132110	133110
197 111	**TW**	SM	*TW*	CH	131111	132111	133111
197 112	**TW**	SM	*TW*	CH	131112	132112	133112

197 113	*	**TW**	SM		131113	132113	133113
197 114	*	**TW**	SM		131114	132114	133114
197 115	*	**TW**	SM		131115	132115	133115
197 116	*	**TW**	SM		131116	132116	133116
197 117	*	**TW**	SM		131117	132117	133117
197 118	*	**TW**	SM		131118	132118	133118
197 119	*	**TW**	SM		131119	132119	133119
197 120	*	**TW**	SM		131120	132120	133120
197 121	*	**TW**	SM		131121	132121	133121
197 122	*	**TW**	SM		131122	132122	133122
197 123	*	**TW**	SM		131123	132123	133123
197 124	*	**TW**	SM		131124	132124	133124
197 125	*	**TW**	SM		131125	132125	133125
197 126	*	**TW**	SM		131126	132126	133126

2. DIESEL ELECTRIC UNITS

CLASS 201/202   PRESERVED "HASTINGS" UNIT   BR

DMBS–TSL–TSL–TSRB–TSL–DMBS.

Preserved unit made up from various Class 201 short-frame cars and Class 202 long-frame cars. The "Hastings" units were made with narrow body-profiles for use on the section between Tonbridge and Battle which had tunnels of restricted loading gauge. These tunnels were converted to single track operation in the 1980s thus allowing standard loading gauge stock to be used. There are nine vehicles that are main line registered and the formation used can be flexible, but at the time of writing it was running in the 7-car formation shown. The set also contains a Class 411 EMU trailer (not Hastings line gauge) and a Class 422 EMU buffet car.

Construction: Steel.
Engine: One English Electric 4SRKT Mk. 2 of 450 kW (600 hp) at 850 rpm.
Main Generator: English Electric EE824.
Traction Motors: Two English Electric EE507 mounted on the inner bogie.
Bogies: SR Mk 4. (Former EMU TSL vehicles have Commonwealth bogies).
Couplers: Drophead buckeye.
Dimensions: 18.40 x 2.50 m (60000), 20.35 x 2.50 m (60116/118/119/528/529), 18.36 x 2.50 m (60501), 20.35 x 2.82 (69337), 20.30 x 2.82 (70262).
Gangways: Within unit only.   **Doors:** Manually operated slam.
Wheel arrangement: 2-Bo + 2-2 + 2-2 + 2-2- + 2-2- + Bo-2 + Bo-2.
Brakes: Electro-pneumatic and automatic air.
Maximum Speed: 75 mph.   **Seating Layout:** 2+2 facing.
Multiple Working: Other ex-BR Southern Region DEMU vehicles.

60000. DMBS. Lot No. 30329 Eastleigh 1957. –/22. 55.0 t.
60116. DMBS. Lot No. 30395 Eastleigh 1957. –/31. 56.0 t.
60118/119. DMBS. Lot No. 30395 Eastleigh 1957. –/30. 56.0 t.
60501. TSL. Lot No. 30331 Eastleigh 1957. –/52 2T. 29.5 t.
60528/529. TSL. Lot No. 30397 Eastleigh 1957. –/60 2T. 30.5 t.

69337. TSRB (ex-Class 422 EMU). Lot No. 30805 York 1970. –/40. 35.0 t.
70262. TSL (ex-Class 411/5 EMU). Lot No. 30455 Eastleigh 1958. –/64 2T. 31.5 t.

| 201 001 | **G** | HD | *HD* | SE | 60116 | 60529 | 70262 | 69337 | 60528 | 60118 | 60119 |
| Spares | **G** | HD | *HD* | SE | 60000 | 60501 | | | | | |

Names:

60000	Hastings	60118	Tunbridge Wells
60116	Mountfield		

CLASS 220   VOYAGER   BOMBARDIER

DMS–MS–MS–DMF.

Construction: Steel.
Engine: Cummins QSK19 of 520 kW (700 hp) at 1800 rpm.
Transmission: Two Alstom Onix 800 three-phase traction motors of 275 kW.
Braking: Rheostatic and electro-pneumatic.
Bogies: Bombardier B5005.
Couplers: Dellner 12 at outer ends, bar within unit.
Dimensions: 23.85/23.00 x 2.73 m.
Gangways: Within unit only.
Wheel Arrangement: 1A-A1 + 1A-A1 + 1A-A1 + 1A-A1.
Doors: Single-leaf swing plug.
Maximum Speed: 125 m.p.h.
Seating Layout: 1: 2+1 facing/unidirectional, 2: 2+2 mainly unidirectional.
Multiple Working: Within class and with Classes 221 and 222 (in an emergency). Also can be controlled from Class 57/3 locomotives.

DMS. Bombardier Bruges/Wakefield 2000–01. –/42 1TD 1W. 51.1 t.
MS(A). Bombardier Bruges/Wakefield 2000–01. –/66. 45.9 t.
MS(B). Bombardier Bruges/Wakefield 2000–01. –/66 1TD. 46.7 t.
DMF. Bombardier Bruges/Wakefield 2000–01. 26/– 1TD 1W. 50.9 t.

220 001	**XC**	BN	*XC*	CZ	60301	60701	60201	60401
220 002	**XC**	BN	*XC*	CZ	60302	60702	60202	60402
220 003	**XC**	BN	*XC*	CZ	60303	60703	60203	60403
220 004	**XC**	BN	*XC*	CZ	60304	60704	60204	60404
220 005	**XC**	BN	*XC*	CZ	60305	60705	60205	60405
220 006	**XC**	BN	*XC*	CZ	60306	60706	60206	60406
220 007	**XC**	BN	*XC*	CZ	60307	60707	60207	60407
220 008	**XC**	BN	*XC*	CZ	60308	60708	60208	60408
220 009	**XC**	BN	*XC*	CZ	60309	60709	60209	60409
220 010	**XC**	BN	*XC*	CZ	60310	60710	60210	60410
220 011	**XC**	BN	*XC*	CZ	60311	60711	60211	60411
220 012	**XC**	BN	*XC*	CZ	60312	60712	60212	60412
220 013	**XC**	BN	*XC*	CZ	60313	60713	60213	60413
220 014	**XC**	BN	*XC*	CZ	60314	60714	60214	60414
220 015	**XC**	BN	*XC*	CZ	60315	60715	60215	60415
220 016	**XC**	BN	*XC*	CZ	60316	60716	60216	60416
220 017	**XC**	BN	*XC*	CZ	60317	60717	60217	60417
220 018	**XC**	BN	*XC*	CZ	60318	60718	60218	60418
220 019	**XC**	BN	*XC*	CZ	60319	60719	60219	60419

220 020	XC	BN	XC	CZ	60320	60720	60220	60420
220 021	XC	BN	XC	CZ	60321	60721	60221	60421
220 022	XC	BN	XC	CZ	60322	60722	60222	60422
220 023	XC	BN	XC	CZ	60323	60723	60223	60423
220 024	XC	BN	XC	CZ	60324	60724	60224	60424
220 025	XC	BN	XC	CZ	60325	60725	60225	60425
220 026	XC	BN	XC	CZ	60326	60726	60226	60426
220 027	XC	BN	XC	CZ	60327	60727	60227	60427
220 028	XC	BN	XC	CZ	60328	60728	60228	60428
220 029	XC	BN	XC	CZ	60329	60729	60229	60429
220 030	XC	BN	XC	CZ	60330	60730	60230	60430
220 031	XC	BN	XC	CZ	60331	60731	60231	60431
220 032	XC	BN	XC	CZ	60332	60732	60232	60432
220 033	XC	BN	XC	CZ	60333	60733	60233	60433
220 034	XC	BN	XC	CZ	60334	60734	60234	60434

Names:

220 009 Hixon January 6th 1968 | 220 016 VOYAGER20

CLASS 221   SUPER VOYAGER   BOMBARDIER

* DMS–MS–MS–MSRMB–DMF (Avanti West Coast or Grand Central units) or DMS–MS–(MS)–MS–DMF (CrossCountry units). Built as tilting units but tilt now isolated on CrossCountry sets.

Construction: Steel.
Engine: Cummins QSK19 of 520 kW (700 hp) at 1800 rpm.
Transmission: Two Alstom Onix 800 three-phase traction motors of 275 kW.
Braking: Rheostatic and electro-pneumatic.
Bogies: Bombardier HVP.
Couplers: Dellner 12 at outer ends, bar within unit.
Dimensions: 23.85/23.00 x 2.73 m.
Gangways: Within unit only.
Wheel Arrangement: 1A-A1 + 1A-A1 + 1A-A1 (+ 1A-A1) + 1A-A1.
Doors: Single-leaf swing plug.
Maximum Speed: 125 mph.
Seating Layout: 1: 2+1 facing/unidirectional, 2: 2+2 mainly unidirectional.
Multiple Working: Within class and with Classes 220 and 222 (in an emergency). Also can be controlled from Class 57/3 locomotives.

* Avanti West Coast or Grand Central units. MSRMB moved adjacent to the DMF. The seating in this vehicle (2+2 facing) can be used by First or Standard Class passengers depending on demand.

Non-standard livery: 221 142 and 221 143 **GC** livery on the driving cars only.

DMS. Bombardier Bruges/Wakefield 2001–02. –/42 1TD 1W. 58.5 t (* 58.9 t.)
60751–794 MS (* MSRMB). Bombardier Bruges/Wakefield 2001–02. –/66 (* –/52). 54.1 t (* 55.9 t.)
60951–994. MS. Bombardier Bruges/Wakefield 2001–02. –/66 1TD (* –/66 1TD). 54.8 t (* 54.3 t.)
60851–890. MS. Bombardier Bruges/Wakefield 2001–02. –/62 1TD (* –/68 1TD). 54.4 t (* 55.0 t.)

DMF. Bombardier Bruges/Wakefield 2001–02. 26/– 1TD 1W. 58.9 t (* 59.1 t.)

Unit										
221 101	*	**VW**	BN	*AW*	CZ	60351	60951	60851	60751	60451
221 102	*	**AM**	BN	*AW*	CZ	60352	60952	60852	60752	60452
221 103	*	**AM**	BN	*AW*	CZ	60353	60953	60853	60753	60453
221 104	*	**AM**	BN	*AW*	CZ	60354	60954	60854	60754	60454
221 105	*	**AM**	BN	*AW*	CZ	60355	60955	60855	60755	60455
221 106	*	**AM**	BN	*AW*	CZ	60356	60956	60856	60756	60456
221 107	*	**AM**	BN	*AW*	CZ	60357	60957	60857	60757	60457
221 108	*	**AM**	BN	*AW*	CZ	60358	60958	60858	60758	60458
221 109	*	**AM**	BN	*AW*	CZ	60359	60959	60859	60759	60459
221 110	*	**AM**	BN	*AW*	CZ	60360	60960	60860	60760	60460
221 111	*	**AM**	BN	*AW*	CZ	60361	60961	60861	60761	60461
221 112	*	**AM**	BN	*AW*	CZ	60362	60962	60862	60762	60462
221 113	*	**AM**	BN	*AW*	CZ	60363	60963	60863	60763	60463
221 114	*	**AM**	BN	*AW*	CZ	60364	60964	60864	60764	60464
221 115	*	**AM**	BN	*AW*	CZ	60365	60965	60865	60765	60465
221 116	*	**AM**	BN	*AW*	CZ	60366	60966	60866	60766	60466
221 117	*	**AM**	BN	*AW*	CZ	60367	60967	60867	60767	60467
221 118	*	**AM**	BN	*AW*	CZ	60368	60968	60868	60768	60468
221 119		**XC**	BN	*XC*	CZ	60369	60769	60969	60869	60469
221 120		**XC**	BN	*XC*	CZ	60370	60770	60970	60870	60470
221 121		**XC**	BN	*XC*	CZ	60371	60771	60971	60871	60471
221 122		**XC**	BN	*XC*	CZ	60372	60772	60972	60872	60472
221 123		**XC**	BN	*XC*	CZ	60373	60773	60973	60873	60473
221 124		**XC**	BN	*XC*	CZ	60374	60774	60974	60874	60474
221 125		**XC**	BN	*XC*	CZ	60375	60775	60975	60875	60475
221 126		**XC**	BN	*XC*	CZ	60376	60776	60976	60876	60476
221 127		**XC**	BN	*XC*	CZ	60377	60777	60977	60877	60477
221 128		**XC**	BN	*XC*	CZ	60378	60778	60978	60878	60478
221 129		**XC**	BN	*XC*	CZ	60379	60779	60979	60879	60479
221 130		**XC**	BN	*XC*	CZ	60380	60780	60980	60880	60480
221 131		**XC**	BN	*XC*	CZ	60381	60781	60981	60881	60481
221 132		**XC**	BN	*XC*	CZ	60382	60782	60982	60882	60482
221 133		**XC**	BN	*XC*	CZ	60383	60783	60983	60883	60483
221 134		**XC**	BN	*XC*	CZ	60384	60784	60984	60884	60484
221 135		**XC**	BN	*XC*	CZ	60385	60785	60985	60885	60485
221 136		**XC**	BN	*XC*	CZ	60386	60786		60886	60486
221 137		**XC**	BN	*XC*	CZ	60387	60787	60987	60887	60487
221 138		**XC**	BN	*XC*	CZ	60388	60788	60988	60888	60488
221 139		**XC**	BN	*XC*	CZ	60389	60789	60989	60889	60489
221 140		**XC**	BN	*XC*	CZ	60390	60790		60890	60490
221 141		**XC**	BN	*XC*	CZ	60391	60791	60991		60491
221 142	*	**0**	BN	*GC*	XW	60392	60992	60986	60792	60492
221 143	*	**0**	BN	*GC*	XW	60393	60993	60994	60793	60493
221 144		**XC**	BN	*XC*	CZ	60394	60794	60990		60494

Names (carried on MS No. 609xx):

221101	101 SQUADRON
221114	ROYAL AIR FORCE CENTENARY 1918–2018
221116	City of Bangor/Dinas Bangor *(alt. sides)*

CLASS 222   MERIDIAN   BOMBARDIER

Construction: Steel.
Engine: Cummins QSK19 of 560 kW (750 hp) at 1800 rpm.
Transmission: Two Alstom Onix 800 three-phase traction motors of 275 kW.
Braking: Rheostatic and electro-pneumatic.
Bogies: Bombardier B5005.   **Dimensions:** 23.85/23.00 x 2.73 m.
Couplers: Dellner at outer ends, bar within unit.
Gangways: Within unit only.   **Wheel Arrangement:** All cars 1A-A1.
Doors: Single-leaf swing plug.   **Maximum Speed:** 125 mph.
Seating Layout: 1: 2+1, 2: 2+2 facing/unidirectional.
Multiple Working: Within class and with Classes 220 and 221 (in an emergency).

222001–004. 7-car units. DMF–MF–MF–MSRMB–MS–MS–DMS.

The 7-car units were built as 9-car units, before being reduced to 8-car sets and then later to 7-car sets to strengthen all 4-car units to 5-cars. 222007 was built as a 9-car unit but later reduced to a 5-car unit. A further reforming programme planned in 2022 saw 7-cars 222005/006 reduced to 5-cars to enable 222 101–104 to be augmented from 4-cars to 5-cars.

DMRF. Bombardier Bruges 2004–05. 22/– 1TD 1W. 52.8 t.
MF. Bombardier Bruges 2004–05. 42/– 1T. 46.8 t.
MSRMB. Bombardier Bruges 2004–05. –/62. 48.0 t.
MS. Bombardier Bruges 2004–05. –/68 1T. 47.0 t.
DMS. Bombardier Bruges 2004–05. –/38 1TD 1W. 49.4 t.

222 001	**EI**	E	*EM*	DY	60241	60445	60341	60621
					60561	60551	60161	
222 002	**EI**	E	*EM*	DY	60242	60346	60342	60622
					60562	60544	60162	
222 003	**EI**	E	*EM*	DY	60243	60446	60343	60623
					60563	60553	60163	
222 004	**EI**	E	*EM*	DY	60244	60345	60344	60624
					60564	60554	60164	

Names (carried on MSRMB):

222 001   THE ENTREPRENEUR EXPRESS
222 002   THE CUTLERS' COMPANY
222 004   CHILDREN'S HOSPITAL SHEFFIELD

222005–023. 5-car units. DMF–MC–MSRMB–MS–DMS (or DMF–MF–MSRMB–MS–DMS).

DMRF. Bombardier Bruges 2003–04. 22/– 1TD 1W. 52.8 t.
MC. Bombardier Bruges 2003–04. 28/22 1T. 48.6 t.
MF. Bombardier Bruges 2004–05. 42/– 1T. 46.8 t.
MSRMB. Bombardier Bruges 2003–04. –/62. 49.6 t.
MS. Bombardier Bruges 2004–05. –/68 1T. 47.0 t.
DMS. Bombardier Bruges 2003–04. –/40 1TD 1W. 51.0 t.

222 005	**EI**	E	*EM*	DY	60245	60347	60625	60565	60165
222 006	**EI**	E	*EM*	DY	60246	60447	60626	60556	60166
222 007	**EI**	E	*EM*	DY	60247	60442	60627	60567	60167

222 008	EI	E	*EM*	DY	60248 60918 60628 60545 60168
222 009	EI	E	*EM*	DY	60249 60919 60629 60557 60169
222 010	EI	E	*EM*	DY	60250 60920 60630 60546 60170
222 011	EI	E	*EM*	DY	60251 60921 60631 60531 60171
222 012	EI	E	*EM*	DY	60252 60922 60632 60532 60172
222 013	EI	E	*EM*	DY	60253 60923 60633 60533 60173
222 014	EI	E	*EM*	DY	60254 60924 60634 60534 60174
222 015	EI	E	*EM*	DY	60255 60925 60635 60535 60175
222 016	EI	E	*EM*	DY	60256 60926 60636 60536 60176
222 017	EI	E	*EM*	DY	60257 60927 60637 60537 60177
222 018	EI	E	*EM*	DY	60258 60928 60638 60444 60178
222 019	EI	E	*EM*	DY	60259 60929 60639 60547 60179
222 020	EI	E	*EM*	DY	60260 60930 60640 60543 60180
222 021	EI	E	*EM*	DY	60261 60931 60641 60552 60181
222 022	EI	E	*EM*	DY	60262 60932 60642 60542 60182
222 023	EI	E	*EM*	DY	60263 60933 60643 60541 60183

Names (carried on MSRMB or DMS):

222 006 THE CARBON CUTTER
222 008 Derby Etches Park
222 015 175 YEARS OF DERBY'S RAILWAYS 1839–2014
222 022 INVEST IN NOTTINGHAM

222 101–104. 5-car former Hull Trains units. Extended from 4-cars to 5-cars in 2022. 222 101/102 DMF–MC–MSRMB–MS–DMS and 222 103/104 DMF–MF–MC–MSRMB–DMS.

DMRF. Bombardier Bruges 2005. 22/– 1TD 1W. 52.8 t.
MC 60571–574. Bombardier Bruges 2005. 11/46 1T. 47.1 t.
MF 60441/443. Bombardier Bruges 2004–05. 42/– 1T. 46.8 t.
MSRMB 60681–684. Bombardier Bruges 2005. –/62. 48.0 t.
MS 60555/566. Bombardier Bruges 2004–05. –/68 1T. 47.0 t.
DMS. Bombardier Bruges 2005. –/40 1TD 1W. 49.4 t.

222 101	EI	E	*EM*	DY	60271 60571 60681 60555 60191
222 102	EI	E	*EM*	DY	60272 60572 60682 60566 60192
222 103	EI	E	*EM*	DY	60273 60443 60573 60683 60193
222 104	**ER**	E	*EM*	DY	60274 60441 60574 60684 60194

CLASS 230 D-TRAIN METRO-CAMMELL/VIVARAIL

The Class 230 D-Train is a DEMU, diesel-battery or battery unit rebuilt from former London Underground D78 Stock by Vivarail. The original D-Train used the bodyshells, bogies and electric traction motors of D78 Stock. Instead of being powered by electricity the motors are instead powered by new underfloor-mounted diesel engines: two per driving car. Modern IGBT electronic controls replaced the previous mechanical camshaft controllers, incorporating automotive stop-start technology and dynamic braking.

230001 was a prototype unit and was followed by 230002, a prototype diesel-battery hybrid that has since been exported to the USA. West Midlands Trains ordered three diesel sets (230003–005) for use on the Bedford–Bletchley Marston Vale Line from spring 2019, but these were stored after Vivarail went into administration in 2022 and have since been and acquired by Great Western Railway. This was followed by an order by Transport for Wales for five 3-car diesel-battery hybrid sets (230006–010) for the Wrexham–Bidston line.

In 2021 original prototype diesel unit 230001 was rebuilt as a fast-charge battery demonstrator unit and it is to be introduced onto the GWR West Ealing–Greenford shuttle in spring 2024.

South Western Railway also has five straight electric sets that it uses on the Isle of Wight (Class 484).

Construction: Aluminium.
Engines/batteries: 230001: 3 x 84kWh Hoppecke batteries in each driving car. 230003–005: 2 x Ford Duratorq 3.2 litre diesel engines of 150kW (200hp) per car. 230 006–010: 4 x Ford Duratorq 3.2 litre diesel engines in centre cars and 2 x 100kWh Hoppecke batteries in each driving car.
Traction motors: TSA TMW 32-43-4 AC motors of 135 kW.
Control System: IGBT Inverter. **Braking:** Rheostatic & Dynamic.
Bogies: Bombardier FLEXX1000 flexible-frame.
Dimensions: 18.37/18.12 x 2.84 m.
Couplers: LUL automatic wedgelock. **Gangways:** Within unit only.
Wheel Arrangement: Bo-Bo + Bo-Bo or to be advised.
Doors: Sliding. **Maximum Speed:** 60 mph.
Seating Layout: Longitudinal or 2+2 facing.
Multiple Working: Within class.

Rebuilt from former London Underground D78 Stock 2016–20. Original D78 numbers are shown alongside the new running numbers.

Class 230/0. Prototype fast-charge battery unit. Refitted with a low density seating layout for demonstration purposes.

DMS(A). Metro-Cammell Birmingham 1979–83. –/28. 38.8 t.
TS. Metro-Cammell Birmingham 1979–83. –/34(+5) 1TD 2W. 20.7 t.
DMS(B). Metro-Cammell Birmingham 1979–83. –/32. 38.8 t.

| 230 001 | **GW** GW | LM | 300001 (7058) 300201 (17058) 300101 (7511) |

Name (carried on 300001): Viva Venturer

Class 230/0. Former West Midlands Trains diesel units. Following Vivarail entering administration in late 2022 these units were taken out of service.

DMS(A). Metro-Cammell Birmingham 1979–83. –/58(+2). 33.3 t.
DMS(B). Metro-Cammell Birmingham 1979–83. –/40(+7) 1TD 2W. 32.3 t.

230 003	**LN**	GW	RG	300003 (7069)		300103 (7127)
230 004	**LN**	GW	RG	300004 (7100)		300104 (7500)
230 005	**LN**	GW	RG	300005 (7066)		300105 (7128)

Class 230/0. Transport for Wales diesel-battery units. Unit weight 99.75 t.

DMS(A). Metro-Cammell Birmingham 1979–83. –/46(+2).
MS. Metro-Cammell Birmingham 1979–83. –/50(+2).
DMS(B). Metro-Cammell Birmingham 1979–83. –/33(+6) 1TD 2W. 35.0 t.

230 006	**TW**	TW	*TW*	BD	300006 (7098)	300206 (17066)	300106 (7510)
230 007	**TW**	TW	*TW*	BD	300007 (7103)	300207 (17063)	300107 (7529)
230 008	**TW**	TW	*TW*	BD	300008 (7120)	300208 (17050)	300108 (7065)
230 009	**TW**	TW	*TW*	BD	300009 (7055)	300209 (17084)	300109 (7523)
230 010	**TW**	TW	*TW*	BD	300010 (7090)	300210 (17071)	300110 (7017)

CLASS 231   FLIRT DMU   STADLER

DMS–TS–PP–TS–DMS. New articulated Transport for Wales FLIRT DMUs for the Cheltenham–Maesteg and Cardiff–Ebbw Vale lines featuring a centre power pack housing diesel engines (with no passenger accommodation in this vehicle) similar to the Greater Anglia Class 755. Air conditioned. Initially in service on the Rhymney Valley line.

Construction: Aluminium.
Engines: Four Deutz V8 of 480 kW (645 hp).
Bogies: Stadler/Jacobs.
Couplers: Dellner 10.
Dimensions: 21.05/15.70/7.20 (PP) m x 2.72.2.82 (PP) m.
Gangways: Within unit.   **Wheel Arrangement:** Bo-2-2-2-2-Bo.
Doors: Sliding plug.   **Maximum Speed:** 90 mph.
Seating Layout: 2+2 unidirectional/facing.
Multiple Working: Within class only.

DMS(A). Stadler Bussnang 2021–22. –/40(+12). 39.5 t.
TS(A). Stadler Bussnang 2021–22. –/52(+10). 24.4 t.
PP. Stadler Bussnang 2021–22. 28.5 t.
TS(B). Stadler Bussnang 2021–22. –/38(+5) 1TD 2W. 25.4 t.
DMS(B). Stadler Bussnang 2021–22. –/40(+12). 39.9 t.

231 001	**TW**	SM	*TW*	CF	381001	381201	381401	381301	381101
231 002	**TW**	SM	*TW*	CF	381002	381202	381402	381302	381102
231 003	**TW**	SM	*TW*	CF	381003	381203	381403	381303	381103
231 004	**TW**	SM	*TW*	CF	381004	381204	381404	381304	381104
231 005	**TW**	SM	*TW*	CF	381005	381205	381405	381305	381105
231 006	**TW**	SM	*TW*	CF	381006	381206	381406	381306	381106
231 007	**TW**	SM	*TW*	CF	381007	381207	381407	381307	381107

231 008	**TW** SM *TW*	CF	381008	381208	381408	381308	381108
231 009	**TW** SM *TW*	CF	381009	381209	381409	381309	381109
231 010	**TW** SM *TW*	CF	381010	381210	381410	381310	381110
231 011	**TW** SM *TW*	CF	381011	381211	381411	381311	381111

Name (carried on both driving cars): 231001   Sultan

3. DMU VEHICLES IN INDUSTRIAL SERVICE

This list comprises DMU vehicles that have been withdrawn from active service but continue to be used in industrial service (such as for use in education establishments or for emergency training).

142033	55574	55624	South Wales Police RFC Ground, Waterton Cross, Bridgend
142043	55584	55634	Sussex Police Training Centre, Kingstanding, near Crowborough
142045	55586	55636	Kirk Merrington Primary School, Co. Durham
144002	55802	55825	The Dales School Blyth
144010	55810	55833	East Lancashire Railway (reserved for Greater Manchester Fire & Rescue)

55801	(ex-144001)	Airedale Hospital, Keighley
55808	(ex-144008)	Fagley Primary School, Bradford
55824	(ex-144001)	Platform 1, Huddersfield Station

4. ON-TRACK MACHINES

These machines are used for maintaining, renewing and enhancing the infrastructure of the national railway network. With the exception of snowploughs all can be self-propelled, controlled either from a cab mounted on the machine or remotely. They are permitted to operate either under their own power or in train formations throughout the network both within and outside engineering possessions. Machines only permitted to be used within engineering possessions, referred to as On-Track Plant, are not included. Also not included are wagons included in OTM consists and overseas based machines that might make occasional short visits.

For each machine its GB operational number, owner or responsible custodian and type is given, plus its name if carried. In addition, for snow clearance equipment the berthing location is given. Actual operation of each machine is undertaken by either the owner/responsible custodian or a contracted responsible custodian.

Machines were numbered by British Rail with either six-digit wagon series numbers or in the CEPS (Civil Engineers Plant System) series with five prefixed digits. Machines delivered from 2013 onwards carry 12-digit EVN series numbers, most additionally carrying a shorter GB operational number. In most cases the later resemble CEPS numbers. Machines are listed here by GB operational number, which in some cases is also the EVN number. Anomalies in such numbering mean this is not strictly numeric, but the order they would have been if allocated CEPS numbers correctly. Machines that carry additional identifying numbers have these shown "xxxx".

(S) after the registered number designates a machine that is currently stored (the storage location of each is given at the end of this section).

DYNAMIC TRACK STABILISERS

DR 72211	BB	Plasser & Theurer DGS 62-N
DR 72213	BB	Plasser & Theurer DGS 62-N

TAMPERS

Plasser & Theurer 09 Series

DR 73109	SK	Plasser & Theurer 09-3X-RT	
DR 73111	SK	Plasser & Theurer 09-3X-Dynamic	
DR 73113	SK	Plasser & Theurer 09-3X-Dynamic	
DR 73114	NR	Plasser & Theurer 09-3X-Dynamic	Ron Henderson
DR 73115	NR	Plasser & Theurer 09-3X-Dynamic	
DR 73116	NR	Plasser & Theurer 09-3X Dynamic	
DR 73117	NR	Plasser & Theurer 09-3X Dynamic	
DR 73118	NR	Plasser & Theurer 09-3X Dynamic	
DR 73120	NR	Plasser & Theurer 09-3X Dynamic	"99 70 9123 120-6"

DR 73121	NR	Plasser & Theurer 09-2X Dynamic	"99 70 9123 121-4"
DR 73122	NR	Plasser & Theurer 09-2X Dynamic	"99 70 9123 122-2"
928001	SK	Plasser & Theurer Unimat 09-4x4/4S Dynamic	"99 70 9128 001-3"
DR 74002	SK	Plasser & Theurer Unimat 09-4x4/4S Dynamic	"99 70 9128 002-1"
DR 75008	CS	Plasser & Theurer 09-4x4/4S Dynamic	"99 70 9123 008-3"
DR 75009	CS	Plasser & Theurer 09-4x4/4S Dynamic	"99 70 9123 009-1"
DR 75010	CS	Plasser & Theurer 09-4x4/4S Dynamic	"99 70 9123 010-9"
DR 75011	CS	Plasser & Theurer 09-4x4/4S Dynamic	"99 70 9123 011-7"
DR 75012	SK	Plasser & Theurer 09-4x4/4S Dynamic	"99 70 9123 012-5"
DR 75013	SK	Plasser & Theurer 09-4x4/4S Dynamic	"99 70 9123 013-3"
DR 75014	SK	Plasser & Theurer 09-4x4/4S Dynamic	"99 70 9123 014-1"
DR 75015	SK	Plasser & Theurer 09-4x4/4S Dynamic	"99 70 9123 015-8"

Names:

| DR 75010 | Roger Nicholas | | DR 75011 | Andrew Smith |

Plasser & Theurer 08 Series and 08 Series (compact)

DR 73803	SK	Plasser & Theurer 08-32U-RT	Alexander Graham Bell
DR 73806	CS	Plasser & Theurer 08-16/32U-RT	Karine
DR 73904	SK	Plasser & Theurer 08-4x4/4S-RT	Thomas Telford
DR 73905	CS	Plasser & Theurer 08-4x4/4S-RT	
DR 73906	CS	Plasser & Theurer 08-4x4/4S-RT	Panther
DR 73907	CS	Plasser & Theurer 08-4x4/4S-RT	
DR 73908	CS	Plasser & Theurer 08-4x4/4S-RT	
DR 73909	CS	Plasser & Theurer 08-4x4/4S-RT	Saturn
DR 73910	CS	Plasser & Theurer 08-4x4/4S-RT	Jupiter
DR 73913	CS	Plasser & Theurer 08-12/4x4C-RT	
DR 73914	SK	Plasser & Theurer 08-4x4/4S-RT	Robert McAlpine
DR 73915	SK	Plasser & Theurer 08-16/4x4C-RT	William Arrol
DR 73916	SK	Plasser & Theurer 08-16/4x4C-RT	First Engineering
DR 73917	BB	Plasser & Theurer 08-4x4/4S-RT	
DR 73918	BB	Plasser & Theurer 08-4x4/4S-RT	
DR 73919	CS	Plasser & Theurer 08-16/4x4C100-RT (with trailer)	
DR 73920	CS	Plasser & Theurer 08-16/4x4C80-RT	
DR 73921	CS	Plasser & Theurer 08-16/4x4C80-RT	
DR 73922	CS	Plasser & Theurer 08-16/4x4C80-RT	John Snowdon
DR 73923	CS	Plasser & Theurer 08-4x4/4S-RT	
DR 73924	CS	Plasser & Theurer 08-16/4x4C100-RT	
DR 73925	CS	Plasser & Theurer 08-16/4x4C100-RT	Europa
DR 73926	CS	Plasser & Theurer 08-16/4x4C100-RT	Stephen Keith Blanchard
DR 73927 (S)	BB	Plasser & Theurer 08-16/4x4C100-RT	
DR 73929	CS	Plasser & Theurer 08-4x4/4S-RT	
DR 73930	CS	Plasser & Theurer 08-4x4/4S-RT	
DR 73931	CS	Plasser & Theurer 08-16/4x4C100-RT	
DR 73932	SK	Plasser & Theurer 08-4x4/4S-RT	
DR 73933	SK	Plasser & Theurer 08-16/4x4/C100-RT (with trailer)	
DR 73934	SK	Plasser & Theurer 08-16/4x4/C100-RT (with trailer)	
DR 73935	CS	Plasser & Theurer 08-4x4/4S-RT	
DR 73936	CS	Plasser & Theurer 08-4x4/4S-RT	
DR 73937	BB	Plasser & Theurer 08-16/4x4C100-RT	

DR 73938	BB	Plasser & Theurer 08-16/4x4C100-RT		
DR 73939	BB	Plasser & Theurer 08-16/4x4C100-RT	Pat Best	
DR 73940	SK	Plasser & Theurer 08-4x4/4S-RT		
DR 73941	SK	Plasser & Theurer 08-4x4/4S-RT		
DR 73942	CS	Plasser & Theurer 08-4x4/4S-RT		
DR 73943	BB	Plasser & Theurer 08-16/4x4C100-RT		
DR 73944	BB	Plasser & Theurer 08-16/4x4C100-RT		
DR 73945	BB	Plasser & Theurer 08-16/4x4C100-RT		
DR 73946	VO	Plasser & Theurer Euromat 08-4x4/4S		
DR 73947	CS	Plasser & Theurer 08-4x4/4S-RT		
DR 73948	CS	Plasser & Theurer 08-4x4/4S-RT		
DR 73949	BB	Plasser & Theurer 08-4x4/4S-RT		"99 70 9123 016-6"
DR 73950	BB	Plasser & Theurer 08-4x4/4S-RT		"99 70 9123 017-4"

Matisa

DR 75301	VO	Matisa B 45 UE		
DR 75302	VO	Matisa B 45 UE		
DR 75303	VO	Matisa B 45 UE	Gary Wright	
DR 75401	VO	Matisa B 41 UE		
DR 75402	VO	Matisa B 41 UE		
DR 75404	VO	Matisa B 41 UE		
DR 75405	VO	Matisa B 41 UE		
DR 75406	CS	Matisa B 41 UE	Eric Machell	
DR 75407	CS	Matisa B 41 UE	Gerry Taylor	
DR 75408	BB	Matisa B 41 UE		
DR 75409	BB	Matisa B 41 UE		
DR 75411	BB	Matisa B 41 UE		
DR 75501	BB	Matisa B 66 UC		
DR 75502	BB	Matisa B 66 UC		
DR 75503	VO	Matisa B 66 UC	"Gill Cowling"	"99 70 9124 001-7"
DR 75504	VO	Matisa B 66 UC		"99 70 9124 002-5"
DR 75505	VO	Matisa B 66 UC		"99 70 9124 003-3"
DR 75506	VO	Matisa B 66 UC		"99 70 9124 004-1"

BALLAST CLEANERS

DR 76501	NR	Plasser & Theurer RM-900-RT	
DR 76502	NR	Plasser & Theurer RM-900-RT	
DR 76503	NR	Plasser & Theurer RM-900-RT	
DR 76504	NR	Plasser & Theurer RM-900	"99 70 9314 504-0"

VACUUM PREPARATION MACHINES

DR 76701	NR	Plasser & Theurer VM80-NR
DR 76703	NR	Plasser & Theurer VM80-NR

RAIL VACUUM MACHINES

99 70 9515 002-2	RC	Railcare 16000-480-UK RailVac OTM
99 70 9515 003-0	RC	Railcare 16000-480-UK RailVac OTM
99 70 9515 004-8	RC	Railcare 16000-480-UK RailVac OTM
99 70 9515 005-5	RC	Railcare 16000-480-UK RailVac OTM

BALLAST FEEDER MACHINE

99 70 9552 020-8	RC	Railcare Ballast Feeder UK

BALLAST TRANSFER MACHINES

DR 76750 NR	Matisa D75		*(works with DR 78802/DR 78812/ DR 78822/DR 78832)*
DR 76751 NR	Matisa D75		*(works with DR 78801/DR 78811/ DR 78821/DR 78831)*

CONSOLIDATION MACHINES

DR 76801	NR	Plasser & Theurer 09-CM-NR
DR 76802	NR	Plasser & Theurer 09-2X-CM "99 70 9320 802-0"

FINISHING MACHINES & BALLAST REGULATORS

DR 77001	SK	Plasser & Theurer AFM 2000-RT Finishing Machine	Anthony Lou Phillips
DR 77002	SK	Plasser & Theurer AFM 2000-RT Finishing Machine	
DR 77010	NR	Plasser & Theurer USP 6000 Regulator "99 70 9125 010-7"	
DR 77322 (S)	BB	Plasser & Theurer USP 5000C Regulator	
DR 77327	CS	Plasser & Theurer USP 5000C Regulator	
DR 77801	VO	Matisa R 24 S Regulator	
DR 77802	VO	Matisa R 24 S Regulator	
DR 77901	CS	Plasser & Theurer USP 5000-RT Regulator	
DR 77903	SK	Plasser & Theurer USP 5000-RT Regulator	
DR 77904	NR	Plasser & Theurer USP 5000-RT Regulator	
DR 77905	NR	Plasser & Theurer USP 5000-RT Regulator	
DR 77906	NR	Plasser & Theurer USP 5000-RT Regulator	
DR 77907	NR	Plasser & Theurer USP 5000-RT Regulator	
DR 77909	NR	Plasser & Theurer USP 5000 Regulator "99 70 9125 909-0"	
DR 77910	CS	Plasser & Theurer USP 5000 Regulator "99 70 9125 008-1"	

TWIN JIB TRACK RELAYERS

DRP 78213	VO	Plasser & Theurer Self-Propelled Heavy Duty
DRP 78215	BB	Plasser & Theurer Self-Propelled Heavy Duty
DRP 78216	BB	Plasser & Theurer Self-Propelled Heavy Duty
DRP 78217 (S)	SK	Plasser & Theurer Self-Propelled Heavy Duty

DRP 78219	BB	Plasser & Theurer Self-Propelled Heavy Duty
DRP 78221	BB	Plasser & Theurer Self-Propelled Heavy Duty
DRP 78222	BB	Plasser & Theurer Self-Propelled Heavy Duty
DRC 78226	CS	Cowans Sheldon Self-Propelled Heavy Duty
DRC 78229 (S)	NR	Cowans Sheldon Self-Propelled Heavy Duty
DRC 78231 (S)	NR	Cowans Sheldon Self-Propelled Heavy Duty
DRC 78234 (S)	NR	Cowans Sheldon Self-Propelled Heavy Duty
DRC 78235	CS	Cowans Sheldon Self-Propelled Heavy Duty

NEW TRACK CONSTRUCTION TRAIN PROPULSION MACHINES

| DR 78701 | BB | Harsco Track Technologies NTC-PW |
| DR 78702 | BB | Harsco Track Technologies NTC-PW |

TRACK RENEWAL MACHINES

Matisa P95 Track Renewals Trains
DR 78801+DR 78811+DR 78821+DR 78831 NR *(works with DR 76751)*
DR 78802+DR 78812+DR 78822+DR 78832 NR *(works with DR 76750)*

RAIL GRINDING TRAINS

Loram C21
DR 79231 + DR 79232 + DR 79233 + DR 79236 + DR 79237	NR
DR 79241 + DR 79242 + DR 79243 + DR 79244 + DR 79245 + DR 79246 + DR 79247	NR
DR 79251 + DR 79252 + DR 79253 + DR 79254 + DR 79255 + DR 79256 + DR 79257	NR
DR 79234 + DR 79235 (S)	NR

Names: DR 79231/237 Pete Erwin *(one plate on opposite sides of each)*
DR 79241/247 Roger South *(one plate on opposite sides of each)*
DR 79251/257 Martin Elwood *(one plate on opposite sides of each)*

Harsco Track Technologies RGH20C
DR 79261 + DR 79271	NR	
DR 79262 + DR 79272	NR	Chris Gibb (on DR 79262)
DR 79263 + DR 79273	NR	
DR 79265 + DR 79264 +DR 79274	NR	
DR 79267 + DR 79277	NR	Bridget Rosewell CBE (on DR 79267)

Loram C44
DR 79301 + DR 79302 +	NR	99 70 9427 038-3 + 99 70 9427 039-1+
DR 79303 + DR 79304		99 70 9427 040-9 + 99 70 9427 041-7
DR 79401 + DR 79402 +	NR	99 70 9427 042-5 + 99 70 9427 043-3+
DR 79403 + DR 79404		99 70 9427 044-1 + 99 70 9427 045-8
DR 79501 + DR 79502 +	NR	99 70 9427 046-6 + 99 70 9427 047-4 +
DR 79503 + DR 79504 +		99 70 9427 048-2 + 99 70 9427 049-0+
DR 79505 + DR 79506 +		99 70 9427 050-8 + 99 70 9427 051-6 +
DR 79507		99 70 9427 052-4

Name: DR 79501 Guy Babbs

RAIL MILLING MACHINES

DR 79101	XR	Linsinger MG31-UK Milling Machine	"99 70 9127 006-3"
DR 79102	NR	Linsinger SF06-UK Milling Machine + trailer DR 79103	"99 70 9127 007-1"
DR 79104	NR	Linsinger SF06-UK Milling Machine + trailer DR 79105	"99 70 9127 008-9"

DR 79601 + DR 79602 +   SC   99 70 9427 063-1 + 99 70 9427 064-9
DR 79603 + DR 79604   99 70 9427 065-6 + 99 70 9527 005-1
        Schweerbau High Speed Milling Machine

STONEBLOWERS

DR 80200 (S)	HR	Pandrol Jackson Plain Line	
DR 80201	NR	Pandrol Jackson Plain Line	
DR 80202 (S)	HR	Pandrol Jackson Plain Line	
DR 80203 (S)	HR	Pandrol Jackson Plain Line	
DR 80204 (S)	HR	Pandrol Jackson Plain Line	
DR 80205	NR	Pandrol Jackson Plain Line	
DR 80206	NR	Pandrol Jackson Plain Line	
DR 80207	HR	Pandrol Jackson Plain Line	99 70 9426 020-2
DR 80208	NR	Pandrol Jackson Plain Line	
DR 80209	NR	Pandrol Jackson Plain Line	
DR 80210	NR	Pandrol Jackson Plain Line	
DR 80211	NR	Pandrol Jackson Plain Line	
DR 80213	NR	Harsco Track Technologies Plain Line	
DR 80214	NR	Harsco Track Technologies Plain Line	
DR 80215	NR	Harsco Track Technologies Plain Line	
DR 80216	NR	Harsco Track Technologies Plain Line	
DR 80217	NR	Harsco Track Technologies Plain Line	
DR 80301	NR	Harsco Track Technologies Multi-purpose	Stephen Cornish
DR 80302	NR	Harsco Track Technologies Multi-purpose	
DR 80303	NR	Harsco Track Technologies Multi-purpose	

CRANES

DRP 81505	BB	Plasser & Theurer 12 tonne Heavy Duty Diesel Hydraulic
DRP 81508	BB	Plasser & Theurer 12 tonne Heavy Duty Diesel Hydraulic
DRP 81513	BB	Plasser & Theurer 12 tonne Heavy Duty Diesel Hydraulic
DRP 81517	BB	Plasser & Theurer 12 tonne Heavy Duty Diesel Hydraulic
DRP 81525	BB	Plasser & Theurer 12 tonne Heavy Duty Diesel Hydraulic
DRP 81532	BB	Plasser & Theurer 12 tonne Heavy Duty Diesel Hydraulic
DRK 81601	VO	Kirow KRC 810UK 100 tonne Heavy Duty Diesel Hydraulic
DRK 81602	BB	Kirow KRC 810UK 100 tonne Heavy Duty Diesel Hydraulic
DRK 81611	BB	Kirow KRC 1200UK 125 tonne Heavy Duty Diesel Hydraulic
DRK 81612	CS	Kirow KRC 1200UK 125 tonne Heavy Duty Diesel Hydraulic

DRK 81613	VO	Kirow KRC 1200UK 125 tonne Heavy Duty Diesel Hydraulic
DRK 81621	VO	Kirow KRC 250UK 25 tonne Diesel Hydraulic
DRK 81622	VO	Kirow KRC 250UK 25 tonne Diesel Hydraulic
DRK 81623	SK	Kirow KRC 250UK 25 tonne Diesel Hydraulic
DRK 81624	SK	Kirow KRC 250UK 25 tonne Diesel Hydraulic
DRK 81625	SK	Kirow KRC 250UK 25 tonne Diesel Hydraulic
DRK 81626	SK	Kirow KRC 250S 25 tonne Diesel Hydraulic "99 70 9319 012-9"

99 70 9319 013-7 NR Kirow KRC 1200UK 125 tonne Heavy Duty Diesel Hydraulic

Names:

| DRK 81601 | Nigel Chester | | DRK 81611 | Malcolm L. Pearce |

LONG WELDED RAIL TRAIN PROPULSION MACHINES

DR 89005	NR	Cowans Boyd PW
DR 89007	NR	Cowans Boyd PW
DR 89008	NR	Cowans Boyd PW

BALLAST SYSTEM PROPULSION MACHINES

DR 92285	NR	Plasser & Theurer PW-RT	
DR 92286	NR	Plasser & Theurer NPW-RT	
DR 92331	NR	Plasser & Theurer PW-RT	
DR 92332	NR	Plasser & Theurer NPW-RT	
DR 92431	NR	Plasser & Theurer PW-RT	
DR 92432	NR	Plasser & Theurer NPW-RT	
DR 92477	NR	Plasser & Theurer PW	"99 70 9310 477-3"
DR 92478	NR	Plasser & Theurer NPW	"99 70 9310 478-1"

BREAKDOWN CRANES

ADRC 96715 (S) NR Cowans Sheldon 75 tonne Diesel Hydraulic

HIGH SPEED 1 MAINTENANCE TRAIN VEHICLES

DR 97001	H1	Eiv de Brieve DU94BA TRAMM with Crane "DU 94 B 001 URS"	
DR 97011	H1	Windhoff MPV (Modular)	
DR 97012	H1	Windhoff MPV (Modular)	Geoff Bell
DR 97013	H1	Windhoff MPV (Modular)	
DR 97014	H1	Windhoff MPV (Modular)	

MOBILE MAINTENANCE TRAINS

Robel Type 69.70 Mobile Maintenance System
DR 97501/601/801 NR "99 70 9481 001-4 + 99 70 9559 001-1 + 99 70 9580 001-4"
DR 97502/602/802 NR "99 70 9481 002-2 + 99 70 9559 002-9 + 99 70 9580 002-2"
DR 97503/603/803 NR "99 70 9481 003-0 + 99 70 9559 003-7 + 99 70 9580 003-0"
DR 97504/604/804 NR "99 70 9481 004-8 + 99 70 9559 004-5 + 99 70 9580 004-8"
DR 97505/605/805 NR "99 70 9481 005-5 + 99 70 9559 005-2 + 99 70 9580 005-5"
DR 97506/606/806 NR "99 70 9481 006-3 + 99 70 9559 006-0 + 99 70 9580 006-3"
DR 97507/607/807 NR "99 70 9481 007-1 + 99 70 9559 007-8 + 99 70 9580 007-1"
DR 97508/608/808 NR "99 70 9481 008-9 + 99 70 9559 008-6 + 99 70 9580 008-9"

ELIZABETH LINE MAINTENANCE TRAIN VEHICLES

DR 97509	XR	Robel Power Car A	"99 70 9481 009-7"
DR 97510	XR	Robel Power Car B	"99 70 9481 010-5"
DR 97511	XR	Robel Power Car B	"99 70 9481 011-3"
DR 97512	XR	Robel Power Car E	"99 70 9481 012-1"

ELECTRIFICATION VEHICLES

DR 76901	NR	Windhoff MPV with Piling Equipment	"99 70 9131 001-8"
DR 76903	NR	Windhoff MPV with Piling Equipment	"99 70 9131 003-4"
DR 76905	NR	Windhoff MPV with Piling Equipment	"99 70 9131 005-9"
DR 76906	NR	Windhoff MPV with Concrete Equipment	"99 70 9131 006-7"
DR 76910	NR	Windhoff MPV with Concrete Equipment	"99 70 9131 010-9"
DR 76911	NR	Windhoff MPV with Structure Equipment	"99 70 9131 011-7"
DR 76913	NR	Windhoff MPV with Structure Equipment	"99 70 9131 013-3"
DR 76914	NR	Windhoff MPV with Overhead Line Equipment	"99 70 9131 014-1"
DR 76915	NR	Windhoff MPV with Overhead Line Equipment	"99 70 9131 015-8"
DR 76918	NR	Windhoff MPV with Overhead Line Equipment	"99 70 9131 018-2"
DR 76920	NR	Windhoff MPV with Overhead Line Equipment	"99 70 9131 020-8"
DR 76921	NR	Windhoff MPV with Overhead Line Equipment	"99 70 9131 021-6"
DR 76922	NR	Windhoff MPV with Final Works Equipment	"99 70 9131 022-4"
DR 76923	NR	Windhoff MPV with Final Works Equipment	"99 70 9131 023-2"

DR 98001	NR	Windhoff MPV with Piling Equipment
DR 98002	NR	Windhoff MPV with Overhead Line Renewal Equipment
DR 98003	NR	Windhoff MPV with Overhead Line Renewal Equipment
DR 98004	NR	Windhoff MPV with Overhead Line Renewal Equipment
DR 98005	NR	Windhoff MPV with Overhead Line Renewal Equipment
DR 98006	NR	Windhoff MPV with Overhead Line Renewal Equipment
DR 98007	NR	Windhoff MPV with Piling Equipment
DR 98009	NR	Windhoff MPV with Overhead Line Renewal Equipment
DR 98010	NR	Windhoff MPV with Overhead Line Renewal Equipment
DR 98011	NR	Windhoff MPV with Overhead Line Renewal Equipment
DR 98012	NR	Windhoff MPV with Overhead Line Renewal Equipment
DR 98013	NR	Windhoff MPV with Overhead Line Renewal Equipment
DR 98014	NR	Windhoff MPV with Overhead Line Renewal Equipment

99 70 9231 001-7	AM	SVI RT250 with crane & access platform
99 70 9231 004-1	AM	SVI PT500 with wire manipulator & access platform
99 70 9231 005-8	AM	SVI RSM9 with access platform
99 70 9231 006-6	AM	SVI RSM9 with access platform
99 70 9231 007-4	AM	APV250 with access platform

Names:

DR 76901	BRUNEL
DR 76923	GAVIN ROBERTS
DR 98003	ANTHONY WRIGHTON 1944–2011
DR 98004	PHILIP CATTRELL 1961–2011
DR 98006	JASON MCDONNELL 1970–2016
DR 98009	MELVYN SMITH 1953–2011
DR 98010	BENJAMIN GAUTREY 1992–2011
DR 98012	TERENCE HAND 1962–2016
DR 98013	DAVID WOOD 1951–2015
DR 98014	WAYNE IMLACH 1955–2015

GENERAL PURPOSE VEHICLES

DR 98215A + DR 98215B	BB	Plasser & Theurer GP-TRAMM with Trailer
DR 98216A + DR 98216B	BB	Plasser & Theurer GP-TRAMM with Trailer
DR 98217A + DR 98217B	BB	Plasser & Theurer GP-TRAMM with Trailer
DR 98218A + DR 98218B	BB	Plasser & Theurer GP-TRAMM with Trailer
DR 98219A + DR 98219B	BB	Plasser & Theurer GP-TRAMM with Trailer
DR 98220A + DR 98220B	BB	Plasser & Theurer GP-TRAMM with Trailer
DR 98307A (S)	CS	Geismar GP-TRAMM VMT 860 PL/UM
DR 98307B*	CS	Geismar GP-TRAMM Trailer
DR 98308A + DR 98308B (S)	CS	Geismar GP-TRAMM VMT 860 PL/UM with Trailer

* In use as a propelling control vehicle at Baglan Bay Yard.

DR 98901 + DR 98951	NR	Windhoff MPV Master & Slave
DR 98902 + DR 98952	NR	Windhoff MPV Master & Slave
DR 98903 + DR 98953	NR	Windhoff MPV Master & Slave
DR 98904 + DR 98954	NR	Windhoff MPV Master & Slave
DR 98905 + DR 98955	NR	Windhoff MPV Master & Slave
DR 98906 + DR 98956	NR	Windhoff MPV Master & Slave
DR 98907 + DR 98957	NR	Windhoff MPV Master & Slave
DR 98908 + DR 98958	NR	Windhoff MPV Master & Slave
DR 98909 + DR 98959	NR	Windhoff MPV Master & Slave
DR 98910 + DR 98960	NR	Windhoff MPV Master & Slave
DR 98911 + DR 98961	NR	Windhoff MPV Master & Slave
DR 98912 + DR 98962	NR	Windhoff MPV Master & Slave
DR 98913 + DR 98963	NR	Windhoff MPV Master & Slave
DR 98914 + DR 98964	NR	Windhoff MPV Master & Slave
DR 98915 + DR 98965	NR	Windhoff MPV Master & Slave
DR 98916 + DR 98966	NR	Windhoff MPV Master & Slave
DR 98917 + DR 98967	NR	Windhoff MPV Master & Slave
DR 98918 + DR 98968	NR	Windhoff MPV Master & Slave
DR 98919 + DR 98969	NR	Windhoff MPV Master & Slave

DR 98920 + DR 98970	NR	Windhoff MPV Master & Slave
DR 98921 + DR 98971	NR	Windhoff MPV Master & Slave
DR 98922 + DR 98972	NR	Windhoff MPV Master & Slave
DR 98923 + DR 98973	NR	Windhoff MPV Master & Slave
DR 98924 + DR 98974	NR	Windhoff MPV Master & Slave
DR 98925 + DR 98975	NR	Windhoff MPV Master & Slave
DR 98926 + DR 98976	NR	Windhoff MPV Master & Powered Slave
DR 98927 + DR 98977	NR	Windhoff MPV Master & Powered Slave
DR 98928 + DR 98978	NR	Windhoff MPV Master & Powered Slave
DR 98929 + DR 98979	NR	Windhoff MPV Master & Powered Slave
DR 98930 + DR 98980	NR	Windhoff MPV Master & Powered Slave
DR 98931 + DR 98981	NR	Windhoff MPV Master & Powered Slave
DR 98932 + DR 98982	NR	Windhoff MPV Master & Powered Slave

Names:

DR 98914+DR 98964	Dick Preston	DR 98923+DR 98973	Chris Lemon
DR 98915+DR 98965	Nigel Cummins	DR 98926+DR 98976	John Denyer

INFRASTRUCTURE MONITORING VEHICLES

"950 001" is a purpose-built Track Assessment Unit based on the BREL Class 150/1 design.

DR 98008	NR	Windhoff MPV Twin-cab with surveying equipment
999600+999601	NR	BREL York Track Assessment Unit "950 001"
999800	NR	Plasser & Theurer EM-SAT 100/RT Track Survey Car
999801	NR	Plasser & Theurer EM-SAT 100/RT Track Survey Car

Name: 999800 Richard Spoors

SNOWPLOUGHS

ADB 965203	NR	Independent Drift Plough	Carlisle Kingmoor Yard
ADB 965206	NR	Independent Drift Plough	Crewe Gresty Bridge
ADB 965208	NR	Independent Drift Plough	Norwich Thorpe Yard
ADB 965209	NR	Independent Drift Plough	Motherwell Depot
ADB 965210	NR	Independent Drift Plough	Carlisle Kingmoor Yard
ADB 965211	NR	Independent Drift Plough	Tonbridge West Yard
ADB 965217	NR	Independent Drift Plough	York Leeman Road Sidings
ADB 965219	NR	Independent Drift Plough	Norwich Thorpe Yard
ADB 965223	NR	Independent Drift Plough	Taunton Fairwater Yard
ADB 965224	NR	Independent Drift Plough	Inverness Millburn Yard
ADB 965230	NR	Independent Drift Plough	Inverness Millburn Yard
ADB 965231	NR	Independent Drift Plough	Motherwell Depot
ADB 965234	NR	Independent Drift Plough	Motherwell Depot
ADB 965235	NR	Independent Drift Plough	Taunton Fairwater Yard
ADB 965236	NR	Independent Drift Plough	Motherwell Depot
ADB 965237	NR	Independent Drift Plough	Tonbridge West Yard
ADB 965240	NR	Independent Drift Plough	York North Yard Sidings
ADB 965241	NR	Independent Drift Plough	Crewe Gresty Bridge

ADB 965242	NR	Independent Drift Plough	Carlisle Kingmoor Yard
ADB 965243	NR	Independent Drift Plough	Carlisle Kingmoor Yard
ADB 965576	NR	Beilhack Type PB600 Plough	Crewe Basford Hall Yard
ADB 965577	NR	Beilhack Type PB600 Plough	Crewe Basford Hall Yard
ADB 965578	NR	Beilhack Type PB600 Plough	Doncaster West Yard
ADB 965579	NR	Beilhack Type PB600 Plough	Doncaster West Yard
ADB 965580	NR	Beilhack Type PB600 Plough	Doncaster West Yard
ADB 965581	NR	Beilhack Type PB600 Plough	Doncaster West Yard
ADB 966098	NR	Beilhack Type PB600 Plough	Doncaster West Yard
ADB 966099	NR	Beilhack Type PB600 Plough	Doncaster West Yard

SNOWBLOWERS

| ADB 968500 | NR | Beilhack Self-Propelled Rotary | Rutherglen OTP Depot |
| ADB 968501 | NR | Beilhack Self-Propelled Rotary | Rutherglen OTP Depot |

ON-TRACK MACHINES AWAITING DISPOSAL

Twin Jib track relayer
DRB 78123 British Hoist & Crane Non-Self-Propelled   Polmadie Down
Holding Sidings

LOCATIONS OF STORED ON-TRACK MACHINES

The locations of machines shown above as stored (S) are shown here.

DR 73927	West Ealing OTM Depot	DR 80202	HNRC, Worksop Depot
DR 77322	West Ealing OTM Depot	DR 80203	HNRC, Worksop Depot
DRP 78217	Glasgow Rutherglen Depot	DR 80204	Dereham, Mid Norfolk Railway
DRC 78229	Land Recovery, Radway Green	ARDC 96715	Nemesis Rail, Burton-upon-Trent
DRC 78231	Land Recovery, Radway Green		
DRC 78234	Land Recovery, Radway Green	DR 98307A	Darley Dale
DR 79234+	LORAM, Derby	DR 98308A+	
DR 79235	LORAM, Derby	DR 98308B	Barry Rail Centre
DR 80200	Dereham, Mid Norfolk Railway		

5. CODES

5.1. LIVERY CODES

AL Advertising/promotional livery (see class heading for details).

AM Avanti West Coast Voyager {interim}. Dark green ends on Virgin Trains silver livery.

AW Arriva Trains Wales or Arriva TrainCare dark & light blue.

CC BR carmine & cream.

CL Chiltern Railways Mainline Class 168 (white & silver).

CR Chiltern Railways (blue & white with a red stripe).

EM East Midlands Trains {Connect} (blue with red & orange swish at unit ends).

EI East Midlands Railway {interim} (white with deep purple swish at unit ends. On Class 222 dark blue window surrounds and grey lower bodyside stripe).

ER East Midlands Railway (purple with white or grey lower bodyside lining and doors).

FB First Group dark blue.

G BR Southern Region/BR DMU green.

GA Greater Anglia (white with red doors & black window surrounds).

GC Grand Central (all over black with an orange stripe).

GW Great Western Railway (TOC) dark green.

LM London Midland (white/grey & green with black stripe around the windows).

LN London Northwestern Railway (light grey, dark green & light green).

NO Northern (deep blue, purple & white).

NR New Northern (white & purple).

O Non-standard (see class heading for details).

SN Southern (white & dark green with light green semi-circles at one end of each vehicle. Light grey band at solebar level).

SR ScotRail – Scotland's Railways (dark blue with Scottish Saltire flag & white/light blue flashes).

ST Stagecoach {long-distance stock} (white & dark blue with dark blue window surrounds and red & orange swishes at unit ends).

SW South Western Railway (two tone grey with a yellow lower bodyside stripe).

TP TransPennine Express (silver, grey, blue & purple).

TW Transport for Wales (white with a broad red stripe at cantrail level & red doors).

VW New Virgin Trains (white with Avanti logos).

WM West Midlands Railway (gold & metallic purple).

XC CrossCountry (two-tone silver with deep crimson ends & pink doors).

5.2. OWNER CODES

A	Angel Trains
AM	Alstom UK
BB	Balfour Beatty Rail Infrastructure Services
BN	Beacon Rail
BR	Brodie Leasing
CO	Corelink Rail Infrastructure
CS	Colas Rail
E	Eversholt Rail (UK)
GW	Great Western Railway
H1	Network Rail (High Speed)
HD	Hastings Diesels
HR	Harsco Track Technologies
LO	LORAM (UK)
LS	Locomotive Services
NR	Network Rail
P	Porterbrook Leasing Company
RC	RailCare UK
SC	Schweerbau (UK)
SG	Swanage Railway
SK	Swietelsky Babcock Rail
SM	SMBC Leasing/Equitix
TW	Transport for Wales
VO	VolkerRail
VT	Vintage Trains
XR	Elizabeth Line

5.3. OPERATOR CODES

AW	Avanti West Coast
CR	Chiltern Railways
CS	Colas Rail
EM	East Midlands Railway
GC	Grand Central
GW	Great Western Railway
HD	Hastings Diesels
LS	Locomotive Services
NO	Northern
SG	Swanage Railway
SN	Southern (part of Govia Thameslink Railway)
SR	ScotRail
SW	South Western Railway
TP	TransPennine Express
TW	Transport for Wales
WM	West Midlands Trains
XC	CrossCountry

5.4. ALLOCATION & LOCATION CODES

Code	Depot	Depot Operator
AK	Ardwick (Manchester)	Siemens
AL	Aylesbury	Chiltern Railways
BD	Birkenhead North	Stadler Rail Service UK
BG	Hull Botanic Gardens	Northern
BQ	Bury (Greater Manchester)	East Lancashire Railway Trust
BY	Bletchley	West Midlands Trains
CF	Cardiff Canton	Transport for Wales
CH	Chester	CAF
CL	Crewe LNWR Heritage	LNWR Heritage Company
CK	Corkerhill (Glasgow)	ScotRail
CY	Crewe South Yard/Gresty Green	*Storage location only*
CZ	Central Rivers (Barton-under-Needwood)	Alstom UK
DY	Derby Etches Park	East Midlands Railway
EP	Ely Papworth Sidings	*Storage location only*
EX	Exeter	Great Western Railway
GA	Gascoigne Wood Sidings (South Milford)	*Storage location only*
HA	Haymarket (Edinburgh)	ScotRail
HD	Holyhead	*Storage location only*
HT	Heaton (Newcastle-upon-Tyne)	Northern
IS	Inverness	ScotRail
LE	Landore (Swansea)	Chrysalis Rail
LM	Long Marston Rail Innovation Centre	Porterbrook Leasing
MA	Longsight (Manchester)	Alstom UK
MN	Machynlleth	Transport for Wales
NH	Newton Heath (Manchester)	Northern
NL	Neville Hill (Leeds)	Northern
NM	Nottingham Eastcroft	East Midlands Railway/Boden Rail
PM	St Philip's Marsh (Bristol)	Great Western Railway
RG	Reading	Great Western Railway
SA	Salisbury	South Western Railway
SE	St Leonards (Hastings)	St Leonards Railway Engineering
SJ	Stourbridge Junction	Parry People Movers
SU	Selhurst (Croydon)	Govia Thameslink Railway
SW	Swanage	Swanage Railway
TM	Tyseley Locomotive Works	Vintage Trains
TS	Tyseley (Birmingham)	West Midlands Trains
WS	Worksop (Nottinghamshire)	Harry Needle Railroad Company
XW	Crofton (Wakefield)	Alstom UK
ZA	RTC Business Park (Derby)	LORAM (UK)
ZB	Doncaster Works	Wabtec Rail
ZD	Derby Works	Alstom UK
ZG	Eastleigh Works	Arlington Fleet Services
ZI	Ilford Works	Alstom UK
ZJ	Stoke-on-Trent Works	Axiom Rail (Stoke)
ZK	Kilmarnock Works	Brodie Engineering
ZN	Wolverton Works	Gemini Rail Group
ZR	Holgate Works (York)	Network Rail